MW00417059

AIM FOR THE
UPRIGHTS

AIM FOR THE UPRIGHTS

The Intentional Playbook for Success in Faith, Family, and Business

STU CRUM

with Douglas Glenn Clark

A Stucrum Publishing Company | Spring, Texas

Published by
A Stucrum Publishing Company | Spring, Texas

Publisher's Cataloging-in-Publication Data
Crum, Stu.

Aim for the uprights : the intentional playbook for success
in faith, family, and business / Stu Crum with Douglas Glenn
Clark. – Spring, TX : A Stucrum Pub. Co., 2024.

p. ; cm.

ISBN13: 978-0-9601249-0-9

1. Success. 2. Faith. 3. Families. 4. Success in business. I. Title.
II. Clark, Douglas Glenn.

BJ1611.2.C78 2024
158.1–dc23

Project coordination by Jenkins Group, Inc. | www.jenkinsgroupinc.com

Interior design by Brooke Camfield

Printed in the United States of America
28 27 26 25 24 • 5 4 3 2 1

CONTENTS

TWO
Game Changer

THREE
Late-Game Score

PREGAME

AIM FOR THE UPRIGHTS

As my student-athlete career ended at the University of Tulsa, my chances of being drafted by the National Football League (NFL) were very good. In my senior year I was ranked third in the nation for field goals, and I played in the Senior Bowl, which in those days was a gateway to professional football. It was the first time my teammates and I got paid to play.

Although I am blessed to have many memorable moments at Tulsa, my goal of turning pro was enhanced in my final year when I kicked four field goals—my best was 57 yards—to beat Oklahoma State, 25–15, in a nationally televised game. I was selected Chevrolet Player of the Game.

Good fortune, to be sure.

But lucky?

I have loved football for as long as I can remember. And from a young age I was an above-average player. There was just one problem: genetics.

My parents, whom I love dearly, did not bless me with height. My mother was barely over 5' tall, and my father was a mere 5'9".

It didn't take long for me to realize that I wasn't going to grow up to be physically intimidating. I would not be tall enough to compete in professional football as a wide receiver, safety, or linebacker. There was only one path to glory: placekicker.

During that Thursday night game against Oklahoma State, most of the television audience did not know that as a 13-year-old, I'd practiced relentlessly, determined to succeed.

In the winter months, I could be found in the basement of my family's home, kicking footballs into a hockey net I'd strung up.

When spring broke, most days you'd find me outside, kicking to improve my strength, form, and accuracy.

From June through August, after working a summer job, six days a week I would go to the local high school and kick footballs. It was a family thing: Dad was my holder; Mom was my retriever: she chased down every ball I kicked so that we could begin another round.

And another.

And another.

Some people who were familiar with my routine may have thought, "My goodness, that young lad has a goal in life."

Looking back, I'd choose a different word—intention.

I intended from a very early age to make the best of my dreams by pushing the limits of my talents and DNA through hard work and a positive attitude.

Regardless, and despite my Tulsa glory days, after 40 years I still hold a number of school records, for points after touchdown percentage, 0.992 (119–120); the two longest FGs, 57 and 58 yards; and most field goals in a season, 21. After years of training and game-day success, I was on the precipice of the next big thing, my dream-come-true scenario: hearing my name called in the NFL draft.

With the other top players in the country, I was invited to attend a number of combines—tryouts, basically—hosted by several teams that wanted an up-close look at that year's draft class.

Then two weeks before draft day, I was contacted by the special teams coach for the New York Giants, who wanted an even closer look at Stu Crum. When I arrived at the Tulsa practice field with my snapper and holder, Coach had already placed 10 footballs on the 30-yard line—a 40-yard field goal—and asked me to kick.

I was ready.

You can do this, Stu. No pressure.

I had my team: a kicker is not a soloist.

My guys know the drill. We've got this.

I took my position, locked in, and began my approach to the ball—

Then Coach surprised me.

"Stu, don't kick it through the goal posts."

I stopped and stared. What?

"I want you to hit the *right* upright," he said.

Why would he ask me to do that? It had no purpose in competition; in fact, all it produced was the thud of disappointment. Also, in that moment, I was quite sure it was impossible to do and I'd fail the audition.

Coach saw the confusion on my face but just smiled and waited patiently for me to digest his request.

I took my position, locked in, and began my approach to the ball.

Everyone watching was amazed, but no one more so than me. That first kick was a winner: the ball clanged against the right upright. I'd done it!

But only that one time. I took nine more kicks, and they all went astray.

Afterward, Coach joined me and pointed to the uprights. "Why do you think I asked you to hit the upright?"

I didn't have a clue and felt lucky to be 1 for 10.

"Stu, I've seen you on film and know your stats. I know you're a good kicker. But I want you to aim higher. I want you to aim for *great* and not just *good*."

It was a profound lesson that would steer me through many significant passages:

- Draft day when I was chosen by the New York Jets.
- Early injury-laden seasons.
- Heart-crushing failure in my first marriage to my high school sweetheart.
- A stint with the Oklahoma Outlaws in the United States Football League.
- That agonizing moment when I realized my professional sports career was over and it was time for Stu Crum to face the next challenge.

Some observers might say that my student-athlete and professional sports career provided special training that has allowed me to excel as a businessman, husband, father, and Christian man of faith. Therefore, they conclude, this focus will not work for people shaped by other experiences.

I disagree.

Every week I write an email to the diverse group of people I work with. I cannot know every challenge they may be facing. But I'm quite sure that my *Stu Speak* encouragements lift all ships in the harbor, because aiming high is universal. And when applied broadly, not just for career, the notion of taking the right aim naturally helps individuals live balanced, well-rounded lives in the face of mounting, impossible demands.

The pages herein include portions of my *Stu Speak* emails. These directives are concise and easy to absorb. But before turning the page, please take a moment to reflect on their impact: Do they hit home? When applied to your aspirations, do they suggest a better or different way to proceed?

More motivational guidance is shared in *The Intentional Playbook*, a project I have developed over several decades of leadership to help men and women further their aspirations by creating strong, clear intentions.

Embracing the *aim for the uprights* concept works for men and women from all walks of life and at every turn in the road because it demands that we aspire to our best intentions. Through it all, may this book be a reminder that success is not measured by our achievements but by the lives we touch.

STU SPEAK

"Following the right path puts you at peace."

ONE

GAME ON

1

MOTIVATING FORCE

" **I**'ve been president for 18 years. When I leave, a change must be made. But because of my personal relationship with people, I can't make those changes. So I'm here to ask you, Stu, if you get this job ..."

The man I would replace at Bridgestone drilled down to the core challenge. If I stepped into his shoes, it would be me who had to reorganize 80 percent of the company's leadership team. These people, who had devoted 30 to 50 years of their lives to the Bridgestone brand, would be facing some drastic changes. And I would not be given a list of names or strategy. No. It would be my responsibility for reviewing regional operations to determine who could help us grow and who could not.

"We need leadership change in this company, Stu. And we need to know that you have the ability to do that."

In the summer of 2013, I retired from Shell Oil Co., where I had thrived for 28 years, eventually serving as chairman and president of Jiffy Lube International. I was 53 years young and eager for new challenges when a headhunter contacted me. I'd been queried in the past, but none of the offers were particularly tempting. The Bridgestone position might be a fine feather in my cap or a nail in my coffin.

Stu, if you get this job . . .

The competitor Stu Crum was all in. In my youth, I was a successful athlete, and I loved to win.

Another part of Stu Crum was anxious. This would be a lot tougher than nailing an extra point or kicking a game-winning field goal. I would no longer have the reliable team I'd enjoyed at Shell. I would be the new guy. The man who must, for the benefit of Bridgestone, deprive successful men and women of a future with the company they loved.

The interview process had been rigorous. The headhunter grilled me before recommending me for the position. Then I met with half a dozen Bridgestone senior-level leaders and took a battery of tests, a strenuous mix of IQ and EQ challenges that measure a person's ability to perceive emotions, think clearly, and manage emotion.

Amid all this analysis, someone might ask, what are they fishing for? How about emotional self-awareness, assertiveness, and independence, to name a few. And then there is stress tolerance—yup, be ready for some super stress in the upper echelons of leadership—as well as empathy and social responsibility, which I'd developed from the time I embraced the philosophy of servant leadership.

Also, as Bridgestone's retail division president retired, the company was simultaneously replacing its chief operating officer.

Intimidating?

A little.

But even though I'd been employed for decades at Shell, that didn't mean my experiences were staid. I did not arrive at the same office all those years. I was stationed around the world, constantly en route to international destinations. Also, in my position with Texaco I was once loaned out, you might say, to a joint venture partner. That's why my new employers saw Caltex, owned by Chevron/Texaco, and Texaco on my curriculum vitae.

Every conscious intention I have made in my life might beg the question, *Can I do this?* In fact, if I don't have a moment of pause or an instance where I've got to suck it up, maybe the intention, in business anyway, isn't daring or deep enough.

Take a moment. Review the consequential decisions you have made. Were you intimidated, just a little? Did your stomach growl or mind roam to disastrous scenarios?

If the only measurement is winning versus losing, we can expect anxiety and doubt to rise in us like a hot blaze. There is a remedy for abating the heat. Define your intentions. Even if you lose momentarily, staying true to the scope of your intentions will set you up for success later.

Yet I confess, whenever I felt a tinge of worry, I would call upon a supportive and reliable coach: my past.

Last in Line

It was embarrassing. Sometimes it made me angry because it happened so often. At 10 years old I was always the last to be selected for team sports.

One summer at church camp we all lined up before a kickball game. Before the two team leaders called any names, my own assessment of my physical stature when compared to the other kids wasn't exactly generous. By then I'd noticed that Mom barely stood 5' tall and Dad's height was only nine inches more. I was the "little kid" at the playground, not a physically intimidating member of my age group, and that would never change.

But I had a secret that buzzed behind my smile. My adversity, a word I did not know at that age, had yielded some compelling results.

Yes, it was frustrating to be overlooked so many times at school and summer camp. It made me want to shout, "Come on, pick me first for once!"

Or defiant, I might think, "I'll show you!" because in all the other group competitions, I had proved that I was a natural athlete, better at sports than most of the other kids who were taller and stronger yet, to be kind, unimpressive. Invariably, by the end of the game—kickball, basketball, baseball, touch football—my value to the team effort was obvious. It was like money in the bank, another concept that had not yet entered my young mind.

Some problems children face will not last. Whatever it is, a parent might say, "You'll grow out of it." Not for me. The genetic deck of cards was stacked against me, so eve   ⁓ adult, I occasionally felt overlooked.

Fast-forward three decades. I'm i
a church softball team. It took sev
first trip to the plate, because I was
rotation. When I finally faced the
20 feet over the home run fence.
my finger at the coach and said.

I was smiling, but I meant   ᵃen
and women, exists. The percep   ᵖect,
became a motivating force at

There is another aspect   about
much until I was at Bridge   ny next
interview: when you are s   ᵉ room,
you can feel like an outsider.

Corporate Wife

At home I wasn't an outsider, despite the millions of miles I logged traveling throughout my career. I had Mia, my wife of 39 years. Some might describe our marriage as traditional: I bring home the paychecks while Mia stays at home with our children. Literally, that is true. But we are collaborators. A husband-and-wife partnership that is strengthened by a shared vision and mutual love for the life we have chosen.

Years before, when I was offered a position in New Zealand, and then Singapore and Latin America, we had to agree that these opportunities were good for the whole family. We were strong because we willingly shared inverse responsibilities. While I climbed the hectic and satisfying corporate ladder to provide for our material needs, Mia conjured the immaterial yet essential ingredient needed for home life—consistency. For our children, yes, but also for husband and wife. I needed her more than ever while interviewing with Bridgestone.

"I can already feel the weight of the responsibility, Mia."

"Me too. All those people . . . the lives you'll change with your decisions."

"Maybe I care too much."

"You're a caring man."

"I know I'll lose sleep. I won't be right—before and after those decisions. And you'll have to live with that as much as me."

"Stu, when we moved to New Zealand, remember the story about the man who noticed my shoes?"

"Remind me."

"He said, 'I've never seen a woman who had shoes that match every outfit.' At first I didn't know how to react. I didn't want to seem materialistic or better than anyone else. But the longer we lived there, I realized that New Zealand life was much simpler and I needed people to know me and know my heart. But this took time.

Stu, when you first meet people, you always say, 'Tell me about your family.' Basically, you're saying, 'Tell me about you.' You don't say, 'How's the job going?'"

"So you're saying—?"

"If you go to Bridgestone, be *you*. Once people feel valued—"

"They open up."

"Get to know the culture, Stu."

THE LISTENING TOUR

Bridgestone leadership had made a shrewd determination. They needed an agent of change whose ties to the past did not exist. In fact, what they were seeking was the quintessential outsider. I was the first executive outside the Bridgestone family to arrive with a mandate: change the mantra, the model, and expand expectations of gain.

But I couldn't swagger into the company like Clint Eastwood. This was not the Wild West. This was an enormous Japanese-owned enterprise that needed fresh insights and economic concepts.

So I scheduled a listening tour.

I traveled a lot in those first months just to get to know the regional divisions and the people within the company. I wanted to hear what everyone thought was going well and where improvements were needed. After all, the departing president didn't give me a to-do list or a playbook. It was my responsibility to assess the current conditions, understand the reasons why change was essential, and develop a dynamic new approach.

Why trust the inner ear of an outsider?

When I played junior varsity football, I was the placekicker. At the start of one game, as I trotted on field to prepare for the kickoff, I noticed the coach from the opposing team sizing me up. Then my ears tingled when I heard him advise his players to move closer. He had assumed that a short player couldn't kick a long ball.

No worries. I didn't curse or complain. I let my ears burn until I finally got a chance to kick a field goal. I crushed a 53-yarder and then listened as that same coach shouted to his players to move back, way back, on the kickoff that followed.

In a sense, I used that same method, my burning ears, to develop my vision for the future of Bridgestone. I didn't sit alone in my office and think stuff up. I let other voices and minds fill my cup. A casual remark, a presumptuous boast, and even some grousing—lots of grousing, actually—could illuminate the playing field.

During my visits with six regional vice presidents, it quickly became clear that each person had a separate way of running the business. They shared the same point-of-sale system, of course, so if you went to a Firestone store or a Tires Plus to make a purchase, the front end was the same. But the way each VP chose leaders, or managed operations or procured parts, for instance, was a little different.

I knew they were very loyal and loved the company. All good people. But their practices were holding back the enterprise, impeding innovation. Set in their ways, they were running the regions like fiefdoms, not as part of one strong company.

I quickly realized that their decentralized decisions were costing Bridgestone a lot of money. We needed to share the same process for buying our oil and parts. A couple of significant changes would add tens of millions of dollars to the bottom line overnight once they were implemented.

I'll give you an example. Imagine 2,200 stores. At each location, if they needed a brake pad, air filter, or oil filter, whatever it was, they could go to their local auto parts store, negotiate the deal, and buy that part.

We needed a new equation. If you slim down from 250 suppliers to four suppliers, which is what we ended up doing, the suppliers we chose would enjoy so much volume they'd gladly give us a better discount. In other words, scale really matters in procurement.

Always ask, why?

Why?

Why were the site managers buying parts in this disorganized manner?

Their suppliers provided perks, like free baseball or football tickets and paraphernalia for doing business with them. It wasn't the best price point for Bridgestone, and it wasn't necessarily the best part. But the managers did it because they had developed personal relationships that they valued.

That's why.

My message—the words of an outsider—didn't sit well with some people, but economy and quality needed to be the cornerstones of our new game plan. *Everyone, we need to put the very best parts in our customers' cars at the best, lowest price.* Our buying power significantly increased when we centralized. I believe we saved close to $20 million just in parts our first year.

Oil procurement was next. We began a conversation with the largest oil suppliers in the United States. We said we'd give them 2,200 stores. But it wasn't just oil we wanted. We needed discounts, marketing programs, and training to make it right for all parties involved. Their cooperation helped bring another $10 million to the bottom line our first year.

I praise everyone involved because no successful business leader is a soloist.

That said, the lucrative changes that we eventually made were made possible, in part, from what I learned during the listening tour.

Well, I admit I also listened to the whispers from a supportive, reliable coach: my past.

Alley Cats

In my previous leadership role, I ran Jiffy Lube. It was a franchise business, so naturally the owners were willing to pool suppliers so that everyone got the best price for supplies. Not that the franchisee was forced to play ball: each made their own decision to join the pool price or search elsewhere for bids.

At times, working with franchisees was a bit like corralling alley cats. Frustrating? Could be. Yet you now know my motivating force: the doubts my physical stature inspired in some coaches, colleagues, and employers fueled my need to succeed at everything I did. The *force* informed my *why*, my reason for being.

But solely using force—a meat cleaver of authority—on others is not my style, nor do I believe it always works or can be sustained. Don't talk to me about Napoleon complex. Honesty, empathy, and faith in myself and the goodwill of others are what have taught me how to succeed, even while working with stray cats, cool cats, and Cheshire cats.

I encourage you to draw on your past.

Equally, I suggest you be cautious: the past can be rocket fuel or concrete boots.

Stu Speak

"A fundamental aspect of experience is its ability to teach resilience. Through each setback, we become stronger and more equipped to face future hurdles with determination and confidence."

THE INTENTIONAL PLAYBOOK

in·ten·tion
[in'ten(t)SHen]
NOUN
   1. a thing intended; an aim or plan

BEING INTENTIONAL: A MINICAMP FOR ROOKIES

Many lives are lived on automatic and therefore rarely soar through the uprights. To be intentional is to be focused, selective, so that the full force of your physical and mental energy flies toward one target.

Think of it as dining out. After browsing the menu, do you order one of everything?

No. You make a selection. By doing so, you are aiming for satisfaction.

The same method, simple as it seems, can be used to create intentional success in all aspects of your life.

PURPOSE

Being intentional includes defining a purpose. As a boy, my one true purpose was to become a successful athlete. Later in life, I selected another purpose: business success. My choices helped me make the most of my time, and I got results.

PRIORITIES

Establishing priorities allows you to take deliberate action toward achieving what you want. Make conscious choices that align with your values, beliefs, and aspirations. Just this much saves you from merely going through the motions or reacting to external circumstances.

DISTRACTIONS

Clear, strong choices automatically filter out distractions. Eliminate unnecessary commitments. Avoid wasting time on activities that do not contribute to your purpose. Priorities pave the way for progress. Dreams and aspirations are achievable.

HARMONY

How does your purpose fit? Revise it if it feels out of sync with your true being and interests. As you progress, you should experience a sense of balance, harmony, and inevitability.

SELF-REFLECTION

Striving for fulfillment is not only about movement and action. Take time to evaluate your thoughts and feelings. Identify areas where you can improve or make changes. Seek to understand your motivations. Overcome limiting beliefs. Self-reflection increases self-awareness and deepens emotional intelligence. Be clear about your progress. Adjust your plans as needed.

RESPONSIBILITY

Decisions have consequences. Be accountable for your outcomes. By doing so, you strengthen the power to shape your own life and avoid being the victim of circumstances beyond your control. Own your results, positive or negative. Intentional living is a social experiment: take notes and learn from mistakes so that you grow from all your intentional experiences.

GRIT

All of the above help you cultivate resilience in the face of challenges. Stay motivated. Forge ahead, rain or shine, as you align each action with your purpose. The result is a deep sense of satisfaction and fulfillment, as you make a meaningful contribution to *your* world, regardless of whether you are pursuing personal growth or professional success.

SMILE

Look at yourself in the mirror. Try to keep a straight face. You will fail. A smile is inevitable. Can't smile? Fake it till you make it. Maintain a positive outlook even in difficult times. Sound a little wacky? Consider the opposite choice.

2

Not Napoleon

In an article published in 2016, a reporter described a new
Bridgestone Vision 2020 store in St. Charles, Illinois, as
"mind-blowing." He was responding to the company's fulfillment
of a mission to create a new type of automotive maintenance shop
that was undeniably customer friendly.

The reporter also quoted Harvey Firestone, the man who
founded the company in 1900. "Our company is built on people—
those who work for us, and those we do business with." In other
words, the goal was always to take care of the loyal customer. At
Bridgetsone we referred to those people as "the boss."

Firestone's comment also implied that employees would be
treated well. Was I living up to the mission statement when six
months into my tenure with Bridgestone I had to let go of eight
loyal employees, some of whom had been with the company for
nearly 40 years?

One angry man I'd had to let go told the world that Stu Crum had destroyed Bridgestone, and that comment would still pain me—a decade later—if not for the positive reviews our two new "Store of the Future" locations received. I was hired to create a new direction, not tread the same old path. As I visited the company's regional fiefdoms, I had to ask myself, "Do I have the right organization in place to deliver great results?" My answer was fast and furious: no!

We needed everyone to come under one flag. The Bridgestone flag. And we could not study only our retail tire and automotive competitors to make good on Vision 2020, a new concept for success.

Can you get an oil change at an Apple store?

Would Nordstrom fit your rig in stylish new tires?

Could Whole Foods or Starbucks add some delicious zip to your sluggish car?

A silly idea, of course. Yet these flourishing customer-oriented companies became our model because most people enjoy those settings, whereas a *USA Today* survey published at the time asked 500 women to name their least favorite activity—and guess what ranked no. 1? "Get my car serviced."

Apparently, her mechanic forgot to offer a caramel macchiato or suggest she browse the designer footwear while waiting for her car to be repaired.

We didn't need to go to extremes to veer into a friendlier atmosphere for drivers of both genders. Yet it was refreshing and a tad audacious to think low-fat strawberry parfait rather than fixate on beating a competitor's price on tire rotation. The money thing is only one thing among many.

Make a silly list of activities or businesses that are clearly outside your realm of expertise. Now ask, do any of them suggest an outrageous adjustment in focus that might alter and improve your best intentions for business, family life, or just plain fun?

If the answer is no, fine! You haven't done any harm by considering new perspectives.

Yet if one preposterous notion tickles your brain or makes you smile, maybe it is worth exploring. Innovation, like the joker in a deck of cards, is always wild.

By the time I was making critical decisions about personnel, I had made a different kind of list. I chose concepts that I believed would announce "game on" in the Bridgestone corporate HQ.

- Increase customer loyalty
- Harness the power of complete auto care
- Build winning markets to grow
- Drive strategic B2B growth
- Establish a high-performance, customer-centric culture

Don't offer free stale coffee in Styrofoam cups on an ugly countertop stained with brown liquid, spilled sugar packets, and a spackle of nondairy creamer product.

Expand the menu. Become a one-stop shop. If customers trust you to replace tires, they might also buy other services—all under one roof.

Offering retail merchandise beyond windshield wipers (T-shirts, branded golf balls, etc.) may have seemed ridiculous back then, but a gift shop is a lot friendlier than a waiting room with a grimy tile floor. And the atmosphere has a dual purpose: serve loyal customers as well as the Bridgestone team members. Lift the mood and intentions of everyone on both sides of the transaction.

SIDESTEPPING WATERLOO

Napoleon Bonaparte, who stood a couple inches above five feet, must have had some good qualities. He was intelligent and had the ability to lead. But his critics described him as a dangerous tyrant who sought absolute rule. As a dictator he was not afraid to wage war despite the thousands of deaths he would incur.

These days, his legacy for some people is the misguided generality that if a man is not tall, he must exert his meaner side to succeed. He will bully anyone who disagrees or blocks his path. Could the opposite be true?

In 2013 I could not lead Bridgestone into a lucrative new arena without being collaborative. Vision 2020 wasn't mine alone; it was created by a team of people who were inspired by the notion that we could expand the tire business if we embraced goodwill, kind customer service, and an expertise that would expand with training.

Going it alone, believing I was the sole savior of an empire, would have led to "my Waterloo," an inference to Napoleon's final defeat at the Battle of Waterloo in 1815 that ended his military dominance in Europe. He was convinced that this one route would erase the memory of his many victories.

On the other hand, in 1963 John F. Kennedy made the bold announcement that America would put a man on the moon in the next decade. Half the people in the room were shocked. They looked at their president and thought, "Are you kidding? The Russians right now are kicking our butt (the Sputnik satellite), and our first space launches were an utter failure. How are we going to do this?"

Kennedy didn't explain. He stood before the American people and said this is our vision; here's what we're going to accomplish. Then, behind closed doors, he had to bring political, business, and NASA along with him. He had to sell his vision. He wasn't a bully.

This was my task at Bridgestone, although I didn't come out of left field and announce a moon shot. Instead, I proclaimed that we are in the "people business," just like Nordstrom and Chick-fil-A, and our goal is to alleviate stress. And we must be consistent, a goal that would depend on how our 23,000 teammates in the shops communicate with customers.

As a leader I had to gain the trust, then build on that and help the team believe in the ideas. Your vision can't just be a word. The leader must live it, be optimistic and even charismatic in his or her pronouncements, and explain why this is important.

Imagine yourself as a member of President Kennedy's team hearing his vision for the first time. How quickly would you buy into this dream? I'm sure Kennedy could be convincing to those who already believed in him. But he would need to expand his legion of believers.

To encourage leadership and management at Bridgestone to fly with me, I began a series of team-building exercises. Sometimes it was as simple as me and Mia hosting dinner at our home, which helped us get to know individuals as well as their spouses or significant others.

I learned during my tenure as president of Jiffy Lube early on that to bring an organization along, you must win the hearts of team members as well as the people they love. Husbands, wives, partners have influence. After all, we all have two lives, right? Work and family. Whatever happens at your job will affect what happens at home. So I recruited family members so they would experience and be part of the process of change. If you get them involved, make them feel part of the new initiative, at times the extended family can become a new leader's allies.

It was the same in football. When I arrived at the University of Tulsa, my first concern was bonding with my snapper and ball holder. Yet those guys already had their own friendships on the team that they could influence. One drop of influence can begin a pool of shared intentions.

That said, like Kennedy and other leaders, once the vision has been established, the leadership team must be given the tools needed to succeed. Funding. Training. Support. Encouragement.

Mr. Bonaparte, your application for employment has been denied.

But why?

Well, Waterloo raises concerns. And, frankly, your EQ scores are rather low.

SOCCER-STYLE STU

Pete Gogolak was the NFL's first soccer-style kicker and played for a couple teams in the 1960s and 1970s. When his family emigrated from Budapest and arrived in upstate New York, his high school didn't have a soccer team, so he adapted and joined the football team.

At the time, it was strange for Americans to see a football kicker approach the ball at an angle and make contact with the instep of his foot, not the toe. Pete's physical stature was also unusual. He wasn't a big, beefy guy who played another position on the team. Like the other European kickers who would make their way to the NFL, he was slender by comparison and had a personality. He disrupted the notion that an athlete had to be physically intimidating to be successful.

Pete played for 11 years in the NFL and was a gateway for other talented players:

- Garo Yepremian (Cyprus)
- Jan Stenerud (Norway)
- Bobby Howfield (England)
- Horst Muhlmann (Germany)
- Toni Fritsch (Austria)

These guys and others were my heroes, but my pro career didn't last long enough, or very long at all, for me to challenge their supremacy.

I was in the first generation of American-born soccer-style kickers drafted in the NFL.

As I gained respect for my kicking skills in high school and then at the University of Tulsa, I was undoubtedly following a trend that is now the standard. But not because soccer kicking was a hip fad and looked cool on the field with its sweeping motion. This method expanded American kickers' accuracy and distance. These days, when an NFL field goal kicker attempts a 50- or 60-yarder, people in the stands hold their breath because there is the real possibility that the player will nail it—and win the game.

In other words, soccer-style kicking became predominant for one reason: results.

I, too, am a result. Of fate.

As a boy, I lived five years in Dallas, where soccer pioneer Lamar Hunt (founder of the American Football League and owner of the Kansas City Chiefs) began a children's soccer league. At the time, I was one of the few American kids who played soccer. What if my parents had moved the family to Houston or Toledo or Seattle? When it came to kicking, soccer was the only style or technique I knew. As I came of age, and watched Pete, Garo, and Jan lift the NFL to new heights in their play every Sunday afternoon, there was no question how I would proceed in my own leagues.

Even so, as I began to compete, I was an outlier. Coaches and teammates accepted my style of play because I could contribute, and everybody pretty much accepted Stu Crum without any teasing or that kind of kid's stuff. Why fight the trend toward soccer-style? If it works.

However, years later as a corporate president, I know too well that change is hard and sometimes it is forced on you. When I was leading Jiffy Lube, we had to expand services because automakers improved their vehicles. In the beginning, an oil change was recommended every 3,000 miles or so. Then it jumped to 10,000. We could not live on oil changes alone.

But convincing franchisees and staff of this necessity? It took patience, and Jiffy Lube was not nearly as large a company as Bridgestone. Anyone interested in knowing more about the roadblocks and complexities associated with making meaningful change will do well to read the perennial best-selling book *Who Moved My Cheese?* by Dr. Spencer Johnson.

In short, some people are better at adapting than others. At Bridgestone, not everyone could get on board. I eventually asked eight senior leaders to step down, but we also lost some middle-level managers because they didn't want to get on the bus. They couldn't buy into the new plan. Or maybe they just couldn't relate to Soccer-Style Stu.

Losing good people may be disappointing. In some measure, we all want acceptance and appreciation. On the other hand, the folks who were on the bus were as excited as I was, and they were delighted that the company was headed to new territory. We were going to the moon, a future that looked bright and boundless.

But not without a lot of time and effort and planning. Maybe JFK took a flyer when he announced his space plan without many details in place to make that happen. At Bridgestone we searched the proverbial sky for new destinations, created a plan, then took our shot.

STU SPEAK

"Behind every victory lies a story of dedication, perseverance, and sacrifice. Winning requires a commitment to excellence and an unwavering desire to succeed."

The Intentional Playbook
Can't Explain

Be unique by refusing to merely follow the crowd or commit to groupthink or a clique. When you follow your true interests, you will attract unique and, at times, inexplicable opportunities.

Back in the day, 45 years ago when I was a high school student, everyone was given a label: freak, jock, nerd, stoner, etc., etc. I hated being told what I was. I only wanted to be me. So I did my own thing—always—and learned how to become my own person.

I stayed on course when I attended the University of Tulsa, pursued a career in professional football, and then became a corporate leader.

Never allow yourself to be put in a box or labeled. *Live a life that can't be explained.*

The "Can't Explain" Game Plan:

- Own your strengths. Bring them to the table. This is the first step to making an impact. Being different and possibly standing alone can be scary. It can also be your greatest asset.

- Diversify. Your greatest strength can become a weakness if you don't explore and develop other personal qualities. Improve your so-called weaknesses. Dare to discover and follow new interests. Find a balance.

- Implement. Getting things done is a prerequisite for becoming a true leader. Start by focusing on tasks and projects that are in your wheelhouse. Do something that will make you shine. Success doesn't happen by accident.

- Shut down critics with a smile. Illuminate negative comments with positive insights. This one intention often reveals the other side of the coin and changes minds without rhetorical arguments.

- Be helpful. Your comrades and critics all want something. Help them get it. It is liberating to willingly allow someone else to take center stage. Keeping the focus only on you and your goals can lead to a sad, lonely existence. Helping others expands your influence and earns you more respect because it is leading by example. Even a small-scale success today can inspire larger-scale victories tomorrow.

- "Never give in. Never, never, never." Winston Churchill also wrote, "Never yield to force; never yield to the apparently overwhelming might of the enemy." On some days, the enemy is a personal doubt or fear. And life can feel unbearable when you feel trapped by a label: Woman. Minority. Immigrant. Too young. Too old. Disabled. Bossy. Weak. *Never give in.*

- Be a person of character and integrity. Doing so will not limit fulfillment. Quite the opposite. Wonderful relationships and influence will follow. There are no shortcuts.

- Savor little everyday moments.

3

X FACTOR

When I was drafted by the New York Jets in 1983, I had fulfilled the dream I'd aimed for since I was a boy. I'll always have that. The memory and the exhilaration.

If my time at the professional level did not go as I had planned, I can still claim the title of the only player to have been on four teams, in two leagues, in the same year. The things you carry to the next phase of life include some tough lessons.

As an athlete, I learned what real pressure is, because there's nothing like standing over a ball with 70,000 people in the stands and 10 million people watching on television with three seconds left in the game. It all comes down to you.

As the clock winds down and the opposing team's stadium fans shout against the hush of suspense, you are at the fulcrum of "the thrill of victory . . . the agony of defeat," the iconic words spoken by Jim McKay every Saturday on ABC's *The Wide World of Sports*.

Emotionally, the victories were incomparable experiences.

I'll never forget the one I lost.

It was late in the game, about a minute left on the clock. I missed a 47-yard field goal, and the disappointment was nearly unbearable. It was a huge game. For my team. For the University of Tulsa. For the fans.

A leader is not invincible. That's one reason I shared this story with my Bridgestone teammates at our first meeting. Another reason was to remind everyone that game-winning kicks are a team effort, not my moment of personal glory. The painful defeats must also be a shared experience; otherwise, the kicker will be a psychological trainwreck every time he faces a live-or-die moment. A placekicker is only as good as the people in front of him. The linemen, the snapper, the holder. No matter the outcome, we share the results.

That philosophy suggests a type of decorum in the chaos of competition.

In my freshman year at Tulsa, we were playing New Mexico State when an embarrassing mishap shook up our team. The ball was snapped just fine, and the holder got his hands around the ball, then accidentally dropped it. I knew I had only one chance to make contact, so I carried through my leg motion and kicked the pigskin before it hit the turf. All I succeeded in doing was drilling the ball into the stands behind our home team bench.

We all felt like the Three Stooges. But as we came off the field, the coach was screaming at me. In the moment, I could have said a lot of things and pointed fingers in defense of myself. Instead, I bore the brunt of rebuke—until Monday when we all gathered to watch the game film. Only then could the coaches dissect what had happened. It was a team mistake, not a Stu Crum blunder. That's when I had one of those "Aha!" moments: team, team, team. We must all carry the weight.

Aiming for the uprights with Bridgestone, even during my challenging but deeply satisfying tenure, wasn't nearly as stressful as missing a kick and losing a big game. However, there was one big difference. Now I had 23,000 teammates who didn't always like me on any given day.

As an athlete, I had the luxury of youth and vast opportunities to learn how to deal with stress.

But these days, how can children cope with all the pressure put on them by well-meaning yet misguided parents?

QUIT TO BEGIN

Early on, I saw that my son, Clayton, had some natural ability. He could hit the ball well as a two-year-old. As an athlete myself, I could tell there was something special about Clayton.

In Texas, never doubt the importance of football. It is a religion. So, no surprise, when Clayton was seven years old, Mia and I decided to sign him up to play peewee football. I was tickled and pleased—until I attended a few practices.

The coaches were treating these little kids like they were 12-, 13-, 15-, and even 18-year-olds. They screamed and yelled with unreasonable expectations. Clayton played one year at that level, and then he quit because it wasn't for him and I disliked the fervor of the coaches we encountered.

Did I just use the word "quit"?

Yes. If you're an athlete at seven, you are still going to be an athlete at 13 or 14.

It wasn't until seventh grade—middle school—that my son played again, and he did well, even though the other kids had been playing peewee for five years.

As a freshman, Clayton faced far more competition on team sports because four middle schools fed into the high school pool of talent, but he had cemented his position as the starting QB of the freshman team. By his sophomore year, he made varsity and was the starting QB as a junior.

Here's my point: Parents, and those coaches in Texas, don't have to push their kids so hard. Not in the beginning. Let young people find themselves. An athlete who has that thing we call the X factor may take unexpected leaps in growth, despite having "quit" and missed some years of play. Their athletic ability will carry them through.

I'm not done.

Let's move to baseball.

Clayton started playing baseball at seven years old and carried through until he turned 12, the years we moved to Miami after I accepted a new position with Shell. That's when he came to me and said, "You know what, Dad—I'm kind of tired baseball. I'm going to stop playing it."

Mia and I were fine with that. "Great. What do you want to do next?"

"I want to play tennis," he said.

By the time we moved back to Texas, when Clayton was 13, he said, "Dad, I miss my buddies in baseball. Let's do baseball again."

And so he quit playing tennis, returned to baseball, and as a freshman—after a two-year layoff because he had burned out—became a starter in the pitching rotation.

In his senior year, as an All-State player, he was drafted by the Chicago Cubs in the Major League Baseball draft. What a quitter!

This scenario won't play out for every boy or girl. And if your children love to play, let them. Becoming a professional athlete is only one goal of many in team sports. I stress that if the talent is there, it may express itself naturally without the parental pressure that can turn a fast, shiny wheel into a flat tire.

My daughter, Katherine, enjoyed a different path. She was a good athlete, but she has the soul of a dancer. She seized her moment in the competitive tryouts for the school drill team—another Texas religion—and by her senior year was named captain of the team that competed throughout the year for honors.

Both my children benefitted from parental support. Yet they succeeded because they both had a burning desire to excel. We must let our children find their path and support their journey.

CLOSE ONE DOOR, OPEN ANOTHER

As a boy, I, too, played various sports. As I grew older, I knew that my first love was football, and so I prepared with the dream intention of becoming a pro.

I loved being the father of an athlete and competitive dancer. I'm sure I share this enthusiasm with dads and moms who are doctors and cheer their children's grasp of science or musicians who can't wait to teach a girl or boy how to play an instrument.

But I was not going to be a father—nor would Mia be the kind of mother—who tried to live vicariously through their kids.

Nor would I be the guy who pushed his kids to do anything they didn't truly want to do, athletically, artistically, or in business. We signed up Katherine for soccer one year, but she didn't like it, so that was the end of that. Close one door, open another.

Despite my hard work and intense focus on my sport, I was cut by the New York Jets in August 1985 during training camp. It was my third year as a professional athlete, yet I'd played only four games, due to injuries and contractual matters.

What to do?

Open another door.

Texaco offered me a six-month training program. I took it and learned every aspect of the business, beginning with pumping gas back when full-service gasoline stations were still around. Mia thought it was hilarious to send her friends so that I could pump their gas. I saw a lot of familiar faces that week.

I also spent time in the credit card center, with supply people, and a week at one of the company's convenience stores.

Sales trainees were expected to learn all aspects of the Texaco system before they were assigned a district marketing manager.

My employer didn't allow me to choose whatever seemed interesting, and if I didn't like one part of the business, I was still required to learn it. So I can't claim the beginning of my business career was like a child experimenting with a lot of different sports. Yet there was one similarity: Clayton, Katherine, and I learned so much from our broad interests. We were generalists. Every competition taught us skills we could, in some way, call upon in our adult years.

When I completed my Texaco training, I was given six company-operated sites. That's where I learned how to run a business with efficiency and empathy. I rose at four o'clock in the morning so that I could meet with the manager at each location before they opened at six. (Twenty-four hour locations were not yet in vogue.)

Learning the business from the ground up was essential. Otherwise, how would I understand the responsibilities of each store manager and know what they were going through each day? By rising before dawn and getting my hands dirty, I developed a strong work ethic and empathy for the players on my team. Not that I was a hand-holder. Everyone was required to do their job, and since I'd learned every detail of the system, I could tell when someone was trying to sell me a stale excuse for mistakes or incompetence.

Mastering the machinations of that type of business gave me a sense of fulfillment when I became a CEO: I could truthfully say I'd done every job in the company.

Stu, can you field a grounder at third base?

Yes, sir.

Distribute the ball on a basketball court?

You bet.

Can you kick a touchdown?

Uh, well, not a touchdown. But as a field goal kicker I'll put a lot of points on the scoreboard.

My effort made me feel secure in my knowledge and skills. It also paid other dividends.

Three years or so into my Texaco employment, the company identified me, and others, as high-potential people, which led to a series of other jobs. The next door that opened for me was a human resources function, where I supported the HR chief.

From there I was moved into the real estate division, where I learned how to assess, buy, and sell real estate in search of prize property and developments. That was big. I learned a lot that would help me decades later.

My next rotation came under the heading of "supply," which meant I was responsible for moving products and supplies through the Texaco pipeline. That was a short stint that prepared me for a very fortunate promotion to a regional leadership position. I managed our St. Louis sites, which required my family to move there. I was 31 years old with a staff that included half a dozen employees who were my father's age.

This may sound like the song that ends with "I did it my way." No way.

As I progressed, it became evermore clear to me that as a business leader I was only as good as the people who surrounded me. My success was dependent on their success. So I remained supportive in every way that I could. That's when I learned that I could be successful only if I became a servant leader.

Also, as a sports or business career begins to ascend, a man or woman might be inclined to go with the flow and see where the momentum takes them. Not me.

As a young athlete I'd assessed my chances of making it to the NFL and adjusted my ambitions and training habits accordingly.

Now as a young man with Texaco, I had to do the same thing. This time I would not be aiming for the NFL; rather, I wanted to be a senior-level executive who managed thousands, if not tens of thousands, of people. I noticed that some people move up through sales, while others rise through marketing or finance. My strategy was to master the details of many different positions and remain a generalist. Why do that? A CEO is a generalist.

Also, merely going with the flow did not suit my need to sharpen my intentions. The various promotions I enjoyed didn't just fall in my lap. I pushed for them.

When I became a regional manager running our sites in three states, global job opportunities would come across my desk. One day I noticed a position in New Zealand.

By then I was 33 years old and had been in the Kansas City position for only a couple years. But I felt a buzz of excitement when I saw the Auckland job description. That night, after our babies were asleep, I sat down with my wife, the mother of our children, my partner.

"Mia, Texaco is a global company. If I ever want to be the top guy, I've got to have global experience."

"I understand. So, we have to move to Europe?"

"I'm thinking New Zealand."

Pause. "You mean the other side of the world?"

Frankly, at the time, I didn't know a lot about New Zealand. Not much about the history, culture, or what it would be like to live there as a family.

"That's a long way from home."

"But it's not a bad place to live, for the kids, for us."

We talked more, and I was ready with some answers. But it was not my style to wait for every last bit of information before making a decision. I explained my strategy to Mia, and we came to an understanding.

"I agree, Stu. Let's look at this opportunity and see what happens."

The next day I put my name in the hat. Days passed. No response from upper management. So I called the managing director in New Zealand, and he began asking questions. We had a good conversation, so I pushed a little more.

"Sir, you don't need to interview anybody else because I'm the right guy for this job. I've got the experience. Fly me to New Zealand and let me interview, because I'm the guy you're looking for."

Is "pushy" an indication of the X factor?

I've come to this conclusion: the X factor usually is found in people who want it more than others. I just wanted it—*bad*. And I let people know how bad I wanted it. Not obnoxious, but I pursued the things that excited me, that I thought I had the talent for.

I did not push for ego gratification or just for the money. I pushed for those opportunities that would give me, Mia, and our children the best possible life. Your intentions may be the expression of your X factor.

But don't go looking for it too soon in your children, or even the young members of your corporate team. I didn't know Clayton was going to be a great athlete. He was a gifted athlete, but I didn't realize he was going to be exceptional until I witnessed the X factor ignite in him.

My X factor was pushing to achieve what was best for my family and business aspirations. Soon this crazy kicker was on his way to New Zealand.

If only I had a Kodak home movie of Stu and Mia on the 20-hour trip. We'd never been on an airplane for so many hours. By the time we landed, we were desperate for sleep. But we were met by Caltex staff who gave us a choice: go to your hotel to sleep or freshen up and come to the office for the interview.

The Crum team seized the moment. Despite not having an ounce of gas left in the proverbial gas tank, we cleaned up at the hotel, then dived into a long afternoon of meetings and interviews with one intention: win the appointment.

We must have done something right, because I was hired and enjoyed a lot of success and a beautiful lifestyle, Mia and I joined a church and volunteered to teach children about faith, and then within a couple years I was promoted to head retail throughout New Zealand.

Shape your intentions.

Believe in yourself even when you may lack a merit badge or two.

Push.

S~TU~ S~PEAK~

"If I couldn't handle being good at something, then how could I consider myself a successful person?"

THE INTENTIONAL PLAYBOOK
SAY YES TO CHANGE

Change is hard to accept because your brain is wired to repeat, repeat, repeat. You may enjoy the perpetual encore for things you like, for better or for worse. You may even accept some habits that are not much fun.

Change upsets all that. Yet positive consequences may follow and can be awesome if you embrace them.

Does this sound like the opposite of intentional? You cannot force life to conform to your list of wants. Intentional means you make choices and intend to walk a certain path regardless of the weather. But if profound change occurs, your intentions may be challenged. You may revise your best intentions.

Your intentional playbook says you are best prepared for change when you recognize that change is always happening. Consider why change is good for you:

YOU ARE PUSHED OUT OF OUR COMFORT ZONE.

Life seems easy when you blindly follow a routine and can predict rewards or consequences. Outside the comfort zone, your assumptions are challenged. Your opinions, mindset, and belief system are tested. You are forced to find new ways to articulate who you are. The simple act of choosing to do something new and different is a friendly act of rebellion. A new approach to life.

YOU EXPERIENCE MORE.

New perspectives don't arrive from outer space. They are waiting at your doorstep. When you look back on your life, most of the memorable moments will have been created by new experiences.

PERSONAL DISCOVERY.

Transitions expand your mind. You learn about your limitations and abundance.

Intentional success is learning who you really are.

MAKES YOU MORE FLEXIBLE AND ADAPTABLE.

Learn to embrace chaos. Make friends with it. Chaos builds confidence. You will flourish in new ways.

MORE FUN.

A man I know was divorced twice before he realized he rarely said yes to new experiences and opportunities. He found the right partner when he commenced what he called the "Year of Saying Yes." Life is fun when it is robust.

4

DEEPEST CUT

Why do some events hurt more than others? Why do they become emotional injuries, a bruise that never quite heals, and not just an outcome on a scorecard?

Although I encourage young people to follow their interests, even if it seems like they are running rampant, playing multiple sports did not always work in my favor.

Senior year in high school was a profound time in my life. I was a three-sport varsity athlete, the starting kicker and free safety on the football team, and I had already accepted a football scholarship to attend the University of Tulsa. I was feeling it. Those early years of defining my intentions and endlessly developing my skills had come to fruition.

Then basketball season came around.

Now, remember, at 5'7" I was never going to be the forward or center, the players who rack up a lot of points. My role was point guard. I was the player who dishes the ball off to the scorers, who had the quickness to make steals and change the momentum of the game. I was a contributor who could help steer the team to success by executing the strategic plan organized by our coaches.

You might say that's also a good way to describe my work as a CEO—a corporate point guard. I distribute instruction, encouragement, mandates, and critical details of our plan to best our competitors in a field of dreams and hard-nosed intentions.

But in high school did I ever think of myself that way? I believed in team play and found it gratifying. Even so, I can't in good faith say that I privately thought, "My sports skills are truly impressive and will likely make me a very successful American business leader."

As a senior, I believed my time had come. As a freshman, I was the starting guard and the same as a sophomore. My junior year was a disappointment because I didn't make the varsity squad, but I kept my starting guard status on junior varsity. As I headed into my final year, Stu Crum was slated to become the starting varsity guard, and everybody knew it. Well, correction: all my teammates, friends, and family members knew it.

But the head basketball coach? Let me be clear: it was *his* decision, not mine. And he had different ideas that year. In his estimation, I likely would not get enough playing time to warrant cutting another player to keep me on the squad.

Also, Coach knew baseball season was right around the corner, and I was the starting center fielder, and the leadoff batter.

So this is how his thinking went: Stu, you're going to play college football. Also, you're a great baseball player, and wouldn't it make more sense for you to prepare for that season? I'm doing you a favor by cutting you from the basketball team so that you can concentrate on baseball and football, because your future is not in basketball—am I right?

For me, a young man who loved to compete, the answer was an emphatic no. I wanted to finish my so-called basketball career with my rightful ascension to point guard. I wanted the joy of playing with my friends on the team—my *best* friends, truth be known—so that we would always look back on our senior year and embellish our shared memories of victory and defeat. Thanks, Coach, you just destroyed my life.

A tad melodramatic, perhaps. But those were my true feelings back then. And it was hard for me, painful, and equally distressing for my family because my father happened to be the president of the booster club. By cutting me from the varsity squad, Coach had put Dad in an uncomfortable position. I still remember my father resigning because his kid wasn't a member of the varsity basketball program. Perhaps that made him look like a poor loser in some people's eyes. In his defense, he was the one who witnessed, day after day, how the deepest cut in my life had made me bleed.

Another memory: Stu Crum crying his eyes out with a sadness that cut to the bone. Little Boy Blue.

The night of the first varsity basketball game of the season I climbed to the very top of the bleachers, where I hoped to hide. I didn't want anybody to notice me, which was ridiculous because everyone at school knew me and my fate. But at least they would all be facing forward once the game began, and this was important because I didn't know how I would react at tip-off. Heaven help me if I began to cry—again.

Tears didn't drop.

Instead, I felt my indignation and frustration rise as I watched my friends lose the game.

Why do some events hurt more than others? Why do they become emotional injuries, a bruise that never quite heals, and not just an outcome on a scorecard?

Four decades later, deep into a career of proud successes, I experienced a similar trauma. My position as chief operating officer at a new company was deemed "unnecessary" and I was dropped from the roster.

The decision to release me was not performance based. It was more along the lines of "We just don't think we need your services at this juncture in the company's growth." Regardless, it was painful. My departure made me feel dispensable, and while it was never spoken, my interpretation of being cut was "You're not good enough."

The next six months were spent swinging at golf balls and invisible demons.

No matter how skilled and experienced you are, a rude bump in the road can fracture confidence. My late-life ordeal matched the impact of being cut from my high school basketball team.

You're not good enough, Stu.

As it turned out, another opportunity came along, and it was a perfect match for me. Had I needlessly wallowed in misery?

A decade after being cut from my basketball team, I returned for a reunion, and guess who also showed up? Coach was gracious as I shared how profoundly painful it was for me to be cut from the team my senior year. Then he offered a saving grace.

"You know, Stu, as I look back on that time, I realize I made a mistake. I never should have cut you. Honestly, I thought I was doing you a favor, but I wasn't. And as it turned out, I didn't do the basketball program any favors either. It's ironic. In my mind I thought I was doing the right thing. If only I could get another chance," he said.

In golf it's called a *mulligan*.

In life it's called regret.

Coach's honesty was a kind of validation for me. We get tossed and turned in a storm, but that shouldn't diminish our sense of self, our confidence. Years before, a man made a decision that pained me, and years later he deemed it a mistake. I felt renewed—until 40 years later when another man, or group of men, in an entirely different environment, cut Stu Crum from the team.

We can't control others. Nor can we predict upheaval, a twist in the road, a heavy wind.

But we can keep our eyes on the uprights. We can learn tough lessons about coping and accepting and still come out on the other side of adversity as a worthy, faithful human being.

STU SPEAK

"Make a conscious effort to smile more throughout the day, even if you don't necessarily feel like it. Practice gratitude and focus on the positive aspects of your life."

THE INTENTIONAL PLAYBOOK
POWER PLAY: FORGIVENESS

The one crucial intention all human beings must foster: learn to forgive.

But how?

Start with empathy, which is the ability to appreciate and share the feelings of others. It is essential for navigating business, family, and faith.

Proceed by understanding that everyone around you is an emotional creature. You, too, are an emotional creature. To be an effective leader, communicator, and problem solver, you must understand emotion.

Emotional intelligence—EQ, not IQ—builds rapport and trust, the essentials of team success.

Like all human skills, empathy can be learned and improved with practice.

Each morning stand in front of a mirror and say, "I intend to forgive."

5

TULSA CONVERSION

The question was kind of weird, and it stunned me.

"If you died today, what are the chances that you'd go to heaven?"

It was 1978, and I was a college freshman, away from home for the first time, hanging out in the dorm with members of the University of Tulsa football team, when a couple of representatives from Campus Crusade for Christ stopped by. Although the question was their way of starting a conversation, the room went quiet for a moment.

I thought it over. Back home, we were a churchgoing family, and I was raised to be kind and generous. I'd always thought of myself as respectful of others, friendly, and willing to lend a hand when asked. But it was the first time anybody had gently provoked me by asking about the hereafter.

"I'd say I have about a 70 percent chance," I said.

Those odds sounded pretty good to me until the visitors began sowing doubts about the wide, unruly gap of 30 percent. What could go wrong? In their opinion, just about anything could tip the scale in favor of hell.

Also, what did I care about immortality? You don't think about those issues a whole lot when you are 18 years old. You assume you'll live forever, or at least 80 years, which seems like forever when you're young. Life after death, if it existed, had better include football, girls, and three meals a day. Not to mention, at the time, my most pressing concern was just making the team. And bonding with my new teammates.

Joe Sandusky, the team's long snapper, was one year ahead of me and a darn good athlete, whose father was a well-known NFL coach. The two of us talked a lot and got along well with the other athletes who would play an important role in our field goal success. Making new friends was fun, but it was also a survival technique: this was my first time away from home, and I was lonely. Homesick. A little lost.

Then a couple weeks into the season, Joe wasn't feeling right. After our Saturday game he complained of symptoms that included shortness of breath. He was coughing and congested. Fortunately, we all had Sunday off and hoped he could get some rest. On Monday, we gathered to watch game film, and though kickers don't have a lot of film to view, I attended with the offensive linemen to see where we could improve as a unit.

Joe never showed up. We learned that he was in the hospital. Pneumonia. That didn't sound good, but it wasn't terminal cancer, and he was 20 years old, a big, strong kid. We assumed he would recover.

He didn't.

On Tuesday, Joe passed away.

His death shook us up, a devastating blow for the entire football program. And it wasn't something we could shake after a few days. The impact felt permanent, like a kick in the head that shatters expectations and assumptions.

The loss threw me. I couldn't process it. I was experiencing all kinds of *firsts* in my life.

First time away from home without the comfort of my parents and brothers.

First year as a Division I athlete in a state that regards football as a religion. The same is true of Texas and Alabama, but I mostly grew up in St. Louis, where football is just a game.

First time to play in a home stadium that could accommodate 42,000 fans. A week later in that season I played for the first time in front of 70,000 people at the University of Arkansas.

First death of a friend, albeit a new friendship, but with a guy who was helping me adjust to college life. There was a big difference between freshman and sophomore year.

There was some guilt, too, but not the *why-him-not-me* variety. I caught myself wondering—a horrible, selfish thought—how I would ever replace my long snapper. From a business perspective, it was a practical concern. But, boy, in the scheme of things, it should have been relegated to 1,000 on my list of worries.

If you died today, what are the chances that you'd go to heaven?

I thought about my conversation with the two guys from Campus Crusade for Christ. At the time, only a month before, their question seemed like a farfetched philosophical riddle. Joe's death brought me into a head-on collision with eternity.

Gee, what *are* my chances? The suddenness and sadness of the situation made my casual "70 percent" guesstimate sound hollow and questionable.

Oh yeah, I'm good.

Final answer?

Then I began suffering from the exact same symptoms that sent Joe to the hospital. I had trouble breathing. It was a psychosomatic disorder, all in my head, and likely spawned by the trauma and stress of loss. It took the comfort and care of more mature teammates to get me through those episodes of panic.

Eddie Hare, a senior, was my holder and a punter who was destined for the NFL. He visited me in my dorm room to talk me down from the ceiling. "Stu, it's going to be okay."

Eddie was a Christian man, as was our starting quarterback, Dave Rader, who came to my aid and was active in the Fellowship of Christian Athletes. Dave would also play in the NFL before becoming a Division I football coach (with a stint at the University of Tulsa) and an Oklahoma state senator.

Our backup quarterback, Bill Blankenship, befriended me as well, and like Dave he was active in the Fellowship of Christian Athletes. In 2009, Bill was named to the Oklahoma Coaches Association Hall of Fame. And last was Joe Blankenship, Bill's younger brother and eventually my roommate in college for three years and for the last 40 years a pastor in Tulsa.

These men were true leaders. They helped Stu Crum, a very young freshman, learn how to take a deep breath, cope, and ask some bigger questions about life.

On the Tulsa campus, the Fellowship of Christian Athletes was called a huddle, but make no mistake, it was a big-tent experience that attracted all of us to find a meaning deeper than sports. They invited me to Bible studies and other FCA meetings, where the talk was always faith based and inspirational. They didn't pressure me in any way, but I began to blitz my muddled beliefs about the afterlife in search of an honest answer to the question, "If you died today _____?"

The inner debate was another first.

A LITTLE WACKY

In March of 1979, after months of mourning the loss of a teammate and questioning who I was at my very core, I experienced an epiphany: it was not good enough to be a *religious* person; I wanted a *relationship*. I made the decision to dedicate my life to Christ. In the end, my choice was not about fear of the afterlife but the joy that comes from having Jesus and the Bible as the compass for my life. A commitment to live well here on Earth, as a moral man whose integrity is not situational.

More than 40 years later, regardless of whether heaven and hell exist (I believe that they do), I tell people that I'm a Christian because my faith in Christ has been my guiding light, through thick and thin. It is not a tedious chore but an intentional, rewarding path that has helped me succeed in business, family life, and, yes, fun.

Criticize me, if you must, and tell me that believing in God makes no sense. At an intellectual level, Christianity does not make any sense. That is what we call faith. Faith is the things unseen.

A little wacky?

Yes, atheists will laugh and tease, as will plenty of other people. But I cannot deny what is in my heart, what drives my being each day, and how my decision has profoundly shaped my life. Someday, when I pass, maybe some observers will say there was something different about that guy Stu Crum.

Whatever. I'm not doing this for show. And I stress: my devotion to Christ is a personal thing. Between me and him.

Do I have friends who don't believe in God? Absolutely. Christians are no better and no worse than anybody else on Earth. We are all God's children—all six billion of us. We all make our own choices about answering the call. We will all fall at one time or another, and we will all need to be picked up and forgiven.

My son doesn't have his dad's faith. He has his own faith and relationship. It's what got him through wretched pain while healing from multiple arm surgeries. My daughter has her own faith too. She calls on it in various ways, big and small. It's a way of life, not a drum we beat.

When Joe died, our coaches dedicated the season to him. He was always in the forefront of our minds, and we did well, finishing with a 9–2 record. Not everyone on the team was a devout Christian. We bonded out of love and respect for Joe and wanted to make him proud of us. His team.

I continue what I call my full-time ministry in business. Throughout my career I've been given the chance to influence thousands of people, not by force but by example. We're all responsible for living the life that God has instructed us to aspire to. Nearly every decision I make passes through my God filter, and there is no need to amend the tenets of my faith to abide by a pressure, imagined or real, to side with the will of an emerging trend.

Today, in 2024, my problem with the Christian faith is that too many of us have forgotten those WWJD bracelets we wore 20 years ago. To some nonbelievers it might seem trite to confront life's challenges by asking, *What would Jesus do?* And yet the question reminds us that Jesus was a simple man who loved and accepted unconditionally. He didn't deride the poor. He put a lot of love on them. Christ is the example of servant leadership.

Mia and I always say that we want to be the hands and feet of Jesus. In other words, rather than just talk a good game, we must live and express his values, the gospel, in everyday life. If we fail that calling, then we have lost our way.

Does that sound a little wacky?

STU SPEAK

"Servant leadership is never motivated by manipulation or self-promotion. In the end, the extent of your influence depends on the depth of your concern for others. That's why it's so important for leaders to be willing to serve."

THE INTENTIONAL PLAYBOOK
PLAYMAKER: FLOW WITH HOPE, NOT HATE

It may seem fashionable and even empowering to use hate as a tactic.

Hate comes in various forms. Fervent and inflexible beliefs, choosing an enemy, joining a group designed to spout rigid, simplistic slogans that leave no room for nuance or paradox.

Hate also makes truth the enemy. Winning becomes the only goal—and by any means possible, including lying and cheating.

Winning is an outcome, not a value. I love to win. But at what cost?

Hope is the opposite of fear and hate. It is not a tactic that aims at an enemy. It is the choice to be confident in your expectations.

Intentions embody hope but with clear marching orders. Urgency, not fanaticism, often accompanies a clear intention.

ARE YOU URGENT?

In my 38 years of professional life, I have observed that some people express a sense of urgency in the way they go about their business, while others are rather ho-hum about most matters.

There are times to be urgent—not rushed—and other times to be reflective.

Yet I believe the most identifiable quality of high-performing men and women is "action orientation." These people have a sense of urgency. They take time to think and plan and set priorities. Then they launch. Launch is a verb:

launch
[lôn(t)SH, län(t)SH]
VERB
  1. set (a boat) in motion by pushing it or allowing it to roll into the water: *"the town's lifeboat was launched to rescue the fishermen"*

Your intentions must launch you and your objectives. Otherwise, what good are they?

Intentions allow you to work steadily, smoothly, and continuously. You will go through enormous amounts of work in the same time that the ho-hum person spends socializing, wasting time, and working on low-value activities.

TEST YOUR INTENTIONS.
How do they feel? When you shape them, write them down, and read them aloud, do you feel a buzz?

When you follow through on your intentions and take on high-value activities, do you enter a mental state called "flow"? Successful people get themselves into this state far more often than their average coworkers.

In the state of "flow"—the highest human state of performance and productivity—something miraculous happens to your mind and emotions. You feel elated and clear because even tough challenges are resolved seemingly without effort. There is also a tremendous sense of calm as you "flow" on a higher plane of creativity and competence.

In my experience you can trigger this state of "flow" by developing a sense of urgency.

Urgency is the natural outcome of defining your intentions.

6

SKILL SET

The Fellowship of Christian Athletes is an international organization with a wide reach and rich history. But any group, large or small, is only as good as its members. I make the distinction because while my attachment and commitment to the FCA is still strong, it all began when I discovered a bunch of very mature, thoughtful individuals who cared about me and understood my struggle after losing Joe Sandusky.

Time, energy, compassion—they gave it all.

Even though I'd been on campus only a couple of months, I quickly decided, "I want to be like these guys. They're good dudes."

Our weekly meetings were held in a large cafeteria on campus. The talks and messages were inspirational and helped me through daily life. I also attended weekly Bible studies, which helped me mature as a young Christian by deepening my understanding of God's word.

Soon I started speaking at local high school gatherings and churches with a group of people who became lifelong friends: Kevin Harlan, Joe Blankenship, and Cliff Abbott. During my time at the University of Tulsa I probably spoke more than 300 times to various groups around the state of Oklahoma, sharing the gospel, but without pressure. Just my story was enough. How I'd come to embrace Christ and how that decision changed my life.

The visits with students were a lot of fun. We sang songs and performed skits, to make it entertaining and enjoyable for the younger people. To this day, those visits during college and afterward are among my fondest memories of the ministry of the Fellowship of Christian Athletes.

But was I practicing to eventually become a minister or pastor?

No. I was developing a skill I didn't know I had.

Through the FCA and the Tulsa football program, I started recognizing my skill set. I was enrolled as a business student and took my courses and all that, but it was public speaking that thrilled me and spawned a new attitude that resulted in my becoming active in business school events.

Every year the University of Tulsa business school announces its choice of Businessman of the Year. They still do it to this day. I know because they invite senior executives from around the country to speak at the award ceremony, and I spoke when I was president of Bridgestone. I was also fortunate enough to have received the award in my senior year.

How did *that* happen?

In truth, I don't know the voting process the dean and professors used. But I suspect I was chosen because I was an above-average student. Despite being active with the FCA, my fraternity Lambda Chi Alpha, and the demands of the football schedule, I hit the books.

Also, I wasn't a wallflower. I was very active in the business school, participating in various department activities. Sometimes just showing up is a special skill.

First and foremost, I believe I was chosen because I was an athlete, and at that time "jocks" were not generally thought to be well rounded.

That's why the business school award was so meaningful: I never wanted to be considered a jock when I was at the University of Tulsa. This may sound like a contradiction coming from the guy who as a boy determined that field goal kicking was his path to success. The truth is the NFL was a dream for me, and I put in the work even though the reality of professional football, a sense of destiny, didn't enter my mind until my junior year at college. Only then did I believe that I might be good enough to be drafted.

So when I arrived on campus my freshman year, I was pondering what I wanted to be when I grew up. More specifically, I wondered what kind of businessperson I wanted to be. That was as big a college focus as kicking a football, because ultimately I never really thought I would make a living kicking a football.

Raising My Game

When I was chosen by Bridgestone Americas to devise and implement big changes in the company's game plan, I was required to travel a lot so that I could meet with employees, shop managers, and regional managers. As president of the retail store group, I would oversee more than 2,200 company-owned stores under the brands of Firestone Complete Auto Car, Tire Plus, Hibdon Tires Plus, and Wheel Works.

I was on the road a lot, gathering information while also assessing conditions and attitudes. Before I could make any decisions about personnel, I needed to do what every politician does during a campaign cycle—meet and greet.

Meanwhile, over a four-month period, I was also meeting at headquarters with Bridgestone leadership to create the new vision—called Vision 2020—that would raise our profile and significantly improve profits within our industry sector.

About six months after my arrival, I brought 3,000 teammates together at a national convention to roll out the playbook. I stood before the audience to announce how the plan would work and why success was dependent on reorganization.

Why am I telling you this?

Everything I've just described falls under the heading of public speaking.

I can draw a direct line from the success I enjoyed as a businessman to what I learned as a speaker in the FCA organization late in my freshman year at Tulsa. The ability to speak to a group of people, large or small, in an arena or in an auto repair garage, raised my game.

Take note: If you wish to move into senior leadership roles, be ready to put yourself in front of audiences. You're the leader, and the people want to hear what the leader has to say. Find your voice and trust it.

If public speaking is not your favorite activity, consider it a risk you must take if you wish to advance. And put it in perspective. Is the fear of standing before an audience larger than making important business decisions?

When we designed a new future for Bridgestone, there was a lot at risk. We were making a major shift from the Transactional Customer, who comes in for a set of tires, to the Lifetime Customer, who returns every time they need an auto repair. Remember, our business models were atypical of our industry and included Starbucks, Apple, Nordstrom, and others. For cars? No, for people. To create devotion, the customer experience needed to be pleasant and respectful, like stopping at your favorite coffee shop or shopping your favorite clothing brand. Could we have fallen flat on our faces? Yes. But standing still was no option.

Learning to speak in public is the same. It's a must. Without learning the skill, a young businessperson is possibly reducing his or her chances of raising the game.

Fortunately, there is no one way to present to an audience. Tailor a method that suits your temperament.

The business world has provided a huge platform for me, and I love sharing with hundreds or thousands of people at a time. The topics vary, and sometimes I still work under the FCA umbrella. In any environment, I love having an impact on other people's lives.

I'm a storyteller, so stories are always the basis for my talks, and I try to bring people into a relaxed, safe place by telling a joke or two. In my experience, the most inspirational speakers are the ones who personalize their message. It's not a lecture. It's not statistics and charts that win the day. I'm aiming for the human heart.

Also, I'm intentionally atypical in my approach to public speaking.

When I was invited to give the commencement speech at the University of Tulsa in 2015—a great honor—I was still chairman and president of Bridgestone Retail Operations, a $4-billion business unit of Bridgestone Americas. Some grads and their families may have expected Mr. Corporate Speaker to stand behind a lectern and deliver a mix of business insights with advice.

Instead, I walked the stage like Chis Rock—without the profanity, of course—and I didn't carry a mic but wore an ear mic, which gave me the freedom to prowl every corner of the stage to reach every sector of the audience. I personalized and physicalized my presentation, pretending to kick a football while sharing my aim-for-the-uprights New York Giants tryout story.

My Tulsa address was an extraordinary opportunity and personally fulfilling. But my methods are the same everywhere I go. My intention is to reveal challenging moments in life as well as triumph. I don't believe inspiration is all about bright, shiny prizes. Reality. Self-deprecation. The realizations we may experience in our darkest hour. These are all welcome ingredients in my storytelling.

I confess: It is fun to be entertaining. If I could tap dance, maybe I'd try that, too, if it would help me relate to my audience or help me to drive home an important point.

Yet none of the speaking I've enjoyed in America and internationally—at times to small groups of leadership personnel—would have happened if I had not been invited to the Tulsa campus FCA gatherings. At that point in my young life, I had never given a public speech, although in high school I was plenty vocal in the locker room. The training I received with the FCA went beyond enriching my understanding of the Bible. Each week I observed a wide range of speakers, each with their own personalities and vocal gifts, and I'd assess—consciously or unconsciously—what was working.

Those opportunities and the impact were a lightning bolt: I loved motivating others.

Put me in, Coach!

STU SPEAK

"We are living in a time when some people care more about winning than about living the truth and having character. Character and integrity matter more to me than making a buck or winning. I love to win—don't get me wrong—but I only enjoy winning by doing it the right way."

THE INTENTIONAL PLAYBOOK
CHOICES

"The only disability in life is a bad attitude."
—Scott Hamilton, Olympic gold medalist

A strong intention is a choice.

Have you ever taken some quiet time to think about the choices you have made in your life? What you might have done differently?

I've thought a lot about the choices I have made over my lifetime and the choices that those around me have made and how they have affected my life.

Whether at work or at home, a single choice (or decision) may have a life-altering effect on you and those around you.

For instance, if a person chooses to drink and drive, they could put their own life and the lives of others at risk. If a teammate chooses to take a shortcut at work, it could result in a safety incident or unintended accident.

There are so many things in life that we can control with the right choices that will lead to a joyful life.

There are just as many things that we can't control in our life. My wife, Mia, was diagnosed with breast cancer 17 years ago. It wasn't her choice.

But she made the choice to do every medical procedure the oncologist recommended to prolong her life.

Her choice was to be aggressive with the procedures and therapies available to her. She also made the choice to be positive throughout the year-long process, despite losing all her hair.

Every day I make a choice to see the glass as half full. Some might choose half empty. My choice means that I treat people with respect and hope to get the same in return.

I aim to be a person of integrity and a man of character. I choose to be part of the solution and not the problem.

What if you make a commitment to help your supervisor or spouse or child but you don't follow through? What are the consequences?

Your intentions have the power to . . .

. . . control more of what happens in life than you might think. Don't be a victim of circumstances. Your choices create your circumstances. We are the players, not the observers of an athletic event.

Own your choices.

Begin thinking about every choice you make and how profoundly the choice creates circumstance.

Then be happy, live well, for you have done your best.

7

Young Love

Wise men say love is blind. Perhaps that is another way of saying young love does not always survive the test of time.

I met Susan the summer before my senior year of high school. She was a sophomore.

Susan and I met and quickly became close.

There were challenges. We went to different high schools, and after graduation her family moved to West Virginia, but the distance did not end our connection. Susan followed me to the University of Tulsa, and we were a couple. She would join me on my speaking engagements for the FCA, and we shared our faith with others.

There were early signs that the relationship wasn't as strong as I had assumed, but I plowed through it. The wise men who said love is blind forgot to add that young love is a little stubborn.

Susan and I married.

Six months later we were divorced. I was shattered and shocked when I realized that my young wife had fallen in love with the president of my football team.

Oklahoma Outlaws

After I was drafted by the New York Jets, my agent and I could not come to a contractual agreement with the team.

Then something miraculous happened. The United States Football League (USFL) came into existence. The USFL was created by businessmen who believed there was an appetite for professional football in the spring and summer, after the NFL and college football seasons had concluded. Even more remarkable, in July real estate mogul William Tatham Sr. announced that he would join the league with the Oklahoma Outlaws.

Initially, Tatham bucked the USFL trend to lease NFL stadiums in large television markets and chose Tulsa because he had family ties in the Sooner State. His team would make its home in the University of Tulsa's Skelly Stadium.

The Outlaws continued to make headlines when team leaders signed Tampa Bay Buccaneers quarterback Doug Williams. Why would such an accomplished player jump from the establishment to the USFL? Apparently, the Bucs didn't want to give Williams a pay raise, so he signed a contract with Oklahoma that made him one of the highest-paid players in professional football.

Obviously, the team needed an excellent quarterback to build a successful franchise. But Bill Tatham Jr., who ran day-to-day operations for the Outlaws and was the owner's son, believed it would be a nice touch—and possibly a sweet marketing ploy—if the team's first signed player was a local athlete. Stu Crum, field goal kicker, was offered a contract.

The Tatham team didn't scrimp. They doubled the Jets' signing bonus offer and significantly increased my salary. Our deal was front-page news in Tulsa.

I was ecstatic. The prospect of playing pro ball for a home-grown crowd thrilled me. Local kid makes good.

And while the money was nice, I was more excited about teaming up with some impressive men. Doug Williams and our general manager, Sid Gilman, legitimized the USFL. Sid is now a member of the NFL Hall of Fame. Doug, the second player to sign with the Outlaws, would join the Washington Redskins in 1986 and two years later become the first African American quarterback to win a Super Bowl.

Doug and I became friends as we toured Oklahoma and nearby Arkansas. The Outlaws' public relations staff put us in front of community groups to build enthusiasm for the brave new world of the USFL and our franchise.

STU SPEAK

"There's a big gap between the life you are living and the life you wish you had. Following your dreams. I support that notion. But just because you're not living your dream life doesn't mean you can't be happy and grateful for the life you have now. This includes the small experiences that we encounter every day. Life isn't always about chasing dreams and living boldly. Sometimes the most joyful, loving, and exciting parts of life are experienced in a single moment."

THE INTENTIONAL PLAYBOOK
CHANGEMAKER: TRUST

Every successful company that I have worked for, every championship sports team that I have played on, and every long-lasting relationship I ever had shared one common denominator: TRUST.

Trust is the cornerstone of any great company, team, or relationship.

To have trust, we need people to make us feel safe, and we must have confidence that they will support us.

Trust is the foundation of relationships because it allows us to be vulnerable without having to be defensive about what we say and do. All great relationships begin and end in trust.

TRUST IS A SHARED BUSINESS INTENTION.
Every successful enterprise, from mom-and-pop store to global corporation, is founded on these traits.

- **Clarity**—People trust the clear and distrust the vague. Communicate clearly and frequently.

- **Compassion**—Think beyond yourself: listen, show appreciation, be engaged, and serve others.

- **Character**—Have high morals and be consistent in your thoughts, words, and actions. Always ask, "Am I doing the right thing?"

- **Competency**—Humility is the first step in learning. Stay competent and capable.

- **Commitment**—Great leadership demands sacrifice. The people who stick with us when things are tough are the ones we can really trust.

- **Connection**—Trust is about relationships. In every interaction we increase or decrease trust. Be genuine, be grateful, and avoid gossip.

- **Contribution**—You must deliver results to be trusted. Give attention, resources, time, opportunity, and help.

Trust your intentions in faith, family, and business.

8

PLAYING HURT

As a young man, a graduate of the University of Tulsa, and a member of the FCA, I was what you would call *legalistic*. Generally, I adhered to laws or formulas, the notion of duty and obligation, which I believed would help me live a good life. They might also limit my compassion for others, but I had not crossed that road yet. Theologically, legalistic meant I leaned toward adherence to moral law rather than a personal set of dos and don'ts.

Unfortunately, my view of life created a troubling dilemma. I considered myself a "good" person compared to those who had succumbed to crime, addictions, or, worse, divorce. Yet as my plane landed in Florida for the Oklahoma Outlaws training camp, I could no longer set myself apart from others. I was now divorced after six months of marriage, and the realization twisted my legalistic viewpoint into a painful knot. I didn't like the category that now defined me. It was embarrassing and humiliating.

So as I embarked on a professional football career—a dream come true—I wasn't only struggling with the emotional trauma of being divorced. I was also fighting the unbearable stain of being somebody whom I never wanted to be, a morally failed man.

There was a solution. It's called mercy. But to receive God's grace, I would need to accept a basic truth: we are all imperfect. I wasn't there yet.

Two weeks into the Outlaws training camp, I tweaked a hamstring muscle that I had torn during my senior year at Tulsa. It brought back memories of another injury that year. In August before every season, the football team endures what we called two-a-days. The team would practice in swelting heat in the morning, then take a noon break, when most guys took a nap or surrendered to an IV drip to restore hydration. Then we'd return in the afternoon for a second workout. It was a grueling schedule for most of the team, but not for kickers. So one day, I decided to play a round of tennis.

All was going well until my opponent hit a wide shot. I dived to return the ball and crashed headfirst into a fence post. It nearly knocked me out, but once I recovered, I didn't think about it much—until the next day on the practice field when I looked up and saw three goal posts.

"This is not good," I told my trainer, who sent me to an optician. The optician sent me to an ophthalmologist, who sent me to a retina specialist, who said, "Stu, you have a detached retina. Did you have a traumatic incident recently?"

Only then did I realize my collision on the tennis court was serious.

Immediate surgery was needed, and I was bummed out because it would mess up my senior year.

I missed the first two games of the season but was given permission to play in the third week against Oklahoma State. Just one problem. My surgeon ordered me to lie low and avoid physical activity until the retina had healed. So when I returned to kick for Tulsa, I was out of shape and tore my hamstring. My season was done. I would graduate the next spring, then return in the fall to begin work on my graduate degree and play my fifth and final year of college eligibility.

Frustrating for me, but what a break for Jason Staurovsky. As a freshman and my backup kicker, he assumed he would not get a chance to play that season. He was called to action and enjoyed an excellent year.

Fate. Fortune. One man's ceiling is another man's floor.

My eyes were just fine in Florida, but the tweaked hamstring negatively affected my kicking because it was my left leg, the one I planted and put all my weight on before swinging my right leg into the ball. The pain was killing me, and my accuracy and distance were poor, but I didn't want to tell the coaches because I couldn't bear losing my wife and my pro career in the same month. I told myself I could play through the pain. I was wrong.

Eventually, I told the coaches why I wasn't kicking the ball as well as they knew I could. They accepted my condition, and I got through training camp and made the team. But even those accomplishments didn't put me in a healthy frame of mind.

As I was mentally distracted and emotionally and physically compromised, my faith became my survival kit. At that point I had nothing else to rely on.

The USFL season finally began, and I played in pain the first four games. I never missed an extra point, but I never made a field goal. In fact, I shouldn't even have attempted a field goal beyond 45 yards. With so little strength in my legs, my kickoffs also began to deteriorate. In college only 23 percent of my kickoffs were returned by the receiver of the opposing team. My pro kicks were so short they provided excellent field position for our competition. Bottom line, Stu Crum was a physical and emotional wreck.

My performance was so poor that the team staff had every right to cut me. I couldn't face that indignity, so I sat down to have a heart-to-heart chat with my head coach.

Woody Widenhofer was, and still is, best known in the National Football League for developing the Pittsburgh Steelers "Steel Curtain" defense that won four Super Bowls in the 1970s. After a stint in the USFL, he became a college coach before returning to the NFL.

Woody was a very nice man, a good man. For that reason, our conversation was fairly easy, and I may have done him a favor by initiating our meeting. We both knew that I wasn't in the right condition, body and soul, to kick at the professional level.

Fans may not fully comprehend the intense pressure that field goal kickers face in those do-or-die moments on the playing field. Throughout high school and college, I took pride in my ability to stay mentally fit and in the moment.

Now, at the threshold of reaching the peak of my profession, my mind was shredded. I couldn't piece it together. Even if my torn hamstring, an injury that takes a long time to recover, was magically healed, I would not have been able to quickly salve the emotional wounds riven by divorce.

The hardest part for me was admitting that my playing days might be over. I never said it out loud. I was a fighter. So Woody and I came to an agreement that allowed me to leave the Outlaws with my pride intact. Sort of.

The next day—literally—it was front-page news in two articles published in the *Tulsa World* newspaper with these two headlines:

OUTLAWS CRUM RETIRES
CRUM: THERE'S LIFE AFTER FOOTBALL, DIVORCE

In *Sports News* a reporter named Charlie Smith summed it up perfectly. "Stu Crum's life seemed perfectly mapped. Marriage to his high school and college sweetheart, a former Miss Teenage America, a professional football player . . ."

I had no quarrel with the coverage. Oddly, I felt supported. The press was very good to me. In Tulsa I'd become a poster boy, a reliable template for the ideal student-athlete who studied hard, played well, and gave back to the community. The press mostly liked me, and I've got to believe they knew the details of my personal life, since the divorce happened in December.

In truth, the chronic hamstring injury, and the emotional turmoil it caused, was plenty to derail my sports career.

But later, after four games in the USFL season when I knew it was time for me to go, I met with the team president, face to face, for a private talk. All I asked was that the Outlaws officially release me from my contract so that I would be free and clear to pursue other opportunities once I was healthy again. Under the circumstances, he agreed it was the right thing to do.

I left that meeting somewhat unburdened from my marital and professional turmoil. I didn't know how my athletic career would play out, but at least I was liberated to play the field.

Then months later, once again fate and fortune put a serious dent in my aspirations.

STU SPEAK

"Nurture your ability to dream great dreams. Think beyond day-to-day realities and find a delicate balance between conceptualization and a daily focus. Be strategic, not just tactical."

The Intentional Playbook
Experience Is What You Get When You Don't Get What You Want

One great thing about getting older is you also become wiser. With age comes experience. Experience is a fascinating aspect of life that shapes our understanding of the world. It encompasses both the joys and the disappointments we encounter along the way.

Often, we set specific goals or have certain expectations, only to find ourselves falling short. However, it is in these moments of not getting what we wanted that we truly learn and grow.

When we don't get what we wanted, it can be easy to feel discouraged, frustrated, and defeated. We may question our abilities or feel like we are not deserving of success.

However, it is important to remember that setbacks and failures are not a reflection of our worth or potential. They are valuable opportunities for growth and self-discovery.

One fundamental aspect of experience is its ability to teach us resilience. In moments of disappointment, we are often faced with challenges and obstacles that test our perseverance. It is during these times that we learn to adapt, to pick ourselves up, and to keep moving forward.

Through each setback, we become stronger and more equipped to face future hurdles with determination and confidence.

Additionally, not getting what we wanted allows us to gain a fresh perspective. When we are fixated on a specific outcome, we may become narrow minded or blinded to alternative possibilities.

When our expectations are not met, we are forced to reevaluate our goals and consider different approaches. This opens the door to new opportunities and allows us to discover paths we may not have otherwise considered.

Experiencing failure or disappointment can also foster humility and empathy. It reminds us that we are not infallible and makes us more understanding of others who may be going through similar struggles. It builds compassion and enables us to offer support and encouragement to those facing their own challenges. By sharing our experiences and offering guidance, we create a community of mutual growth and understanding.

Failure provides an opportunity to reassess values, passions, and ambitions and make adjustments accordingly. It allows us to align our goals with our authentic selves, leading to a more fulfilling and purposeful life.

Also, not getting what we wanted teaches us the value of patience and perseverance. In a world that often emphasizes instant gratification, experiencing setbacks can be frustrating. It is through patience that we develop the resilience and determination needed to overcome obstacles.

Experience is what we gain when our expectations are not met.

TWO

GAME
CHANGER

9

SECOND WIND

I returned to Tulsa in the spring of 1984 with the goal of just trying to get healthy and stay busy. The University of Tulsa's admission department hired me to recruit high school students, which allowed me to attend various scholastic events, travel a bit, and put my public speaking skills to work.

By September, I was also the sideline radio commentator for Tulsa football games. I roamed the sidelines interviewing players and others, providing a kind of play-by-play of activities, injuries, and whatever else was happening during the games. I also traveled with the team the entire fall.

On the outside I was smiling, happy Stu. On the inside I was still churning, troubled by the circumstances of a divorce and faltering in professional sports. Within me a stranger had arrived, and he brought something to my social interactions that was unfamiliar: I was wary. Mostly of women.

Then I was introduced to Mia.

Although she was a student at Westminster College in Missouri, Mia was visiting a friend and her sister, Madeleine, in Tulsa, and they attended a football game. While in the stands, Mia's friend pointed to the sideline reporter and said, "You see that guy down there? I think you'd really get along. You have similar personalities. You should meet him."

Mia agreed to meet me.

Our talk after the game was friendly and memorable. I was so charmed I called my parents that night and said, "Mom, Dad, I know you're going to think this sounds crazy, but I just met a girl who makes me want to get married again."

They were encouraging.

Luck was on my side. In the coming weeks, my recruiting work for the University of Tulsa would take me to Columbia, Missouri, a short distance from Fulton, Mia's college town.

On our first date, I picked her up at her dorm and took her to dinner. We both quickly knew that there was an attraction, yes, but also a meeting of minds, spirit, and faith.

We discussed the things that really mattered to us, and all the blinders were removed. We agreed that life wasn't about being perfect, and so I could essentially say, "Here are my troubles," and then expand from there. After all, I couldn't hide my divorce. The long shadow it cast would catch up to me sooner or later. So we discussed its impact, the shame I felt, and how I feared it tainted me.

Later, Mia would tell me that she felt my marital downfall had likely strengthened my character, not damaged it. "When you go through hardship, you have to look into yourself. You become a man." She went further, suggesting that Susan had married the "boy" Stu Crum. But the woman in his next meaningful relationship would marry "the man."

Mia was wise for her years. She could tell that heartbreak was one thing, but even worse, the divorce was a blow to my ego and therefore would naturally make me question the future that was now sprinkled with personal doubts.

On the many dates that followed, our love grew. We agreed that all blessings come from God, and therefore we would share our good fortune with others. What flows in must flow out.

If Mia and I immediately knew we were a match, we also knew we had a couple obstacles to overcome. I thought the stigma of my divorce was a family issue because Mia's father was a minister.

Oh, Dad, I'm dating this great divorced guy.

That's not a conversation any daughter wants to have with her parents.

What I soon realized is they would love and accept me just as I am because her parents were strong believers in Christ, his unconditional love, and most importantly the meaning of grace.

There was one more river to cross.

What kind of work do you do, Stu?

Mr. Football

Mia met me on the sidelines of a Tulsa football game, so she had some sense of my professional interests, while at the same time she was mindful that the gridiron commentary was seasonal. On our first date she asked the big question.

"What's your job?"

"I play football."

"No, I mean, what's your *real* job?"

"Well, I play football."

Mia was not raised in a household that gathered around the television every weekend to cheer NFL teams. Her parents, who immigrated from Germany, no surprise, liked soccer.

"Well, no, I understand you like to kick a football, but what's your—?"

"My real job is football," I said with a smile.

It's all a hoot because 40 years later, on any given Sunday, you might find me puttering in the garden while Mia is watching a Kansas City Chiefs game.

Back in the day, I had not given up on pro football but may have entertained occasional private thoughts about finally retiring as Mia and I continued to date and talk about our future.

Then the phone rang. It was late summer 1984, and my agent had been trolling the NFL looking for opportunities since the Oklahoma Outlaws had released me. I was still in the league's database when he discovered that the Kansas City Chiefs were in a bind.

The organization had an exceptional kicker in Nick Lowery. He was All-Pro. But Nick had undergone a preseason surgery and would need four or five games to recover. They had to find a kicker who could fill in until Nick was healthy again.

As it turned out, the New York Jets still owned my NFL rights even though I had never signed a contract with them. Regardless, they agreed to trade me—a twelfth-round draft choice—to the Kansas City Chiefs for a tenth-round draft choice. I thought it was pretty cool that my value had increased by moving up two draft picks.

The Chiefs flew me out for a tryout during their training camp. I kicked about 50 balls and never missed one. I was healthy again and mentally fit.

About a week into my time with Kansas City, I was going to be the starting kicker and poised to begin the NFL season. Then my agent got a call from the attorney for the Chicago Blitz of the USFL.

"Sorry," he said, "but Stu can't kick for the Chiefs because we picked him up on waivers when he left the Outlaws. We just hadn't told him."

Marv Levy, who is best known for a long career with the Buffalo Bills, was the Chicago Blitz coach. When the dispute with Kansas City exploded, I spoke with Marv and all but begged him to let me stay with the Chiefs so that I could play in the NFL.

"Stu," he said, "we need a great kicker, and we think you're perfect for the organization."

That began a legal battle that put me in limbo—in Kansas City—as the season was about to begin. Lawyers from both leagues squabbled about who owned Stu Crum. When it was determined that I was still the property of the United States Football League, I told my agent about the agreement I had ironed out with Bill Tatham Jr. The president of operations had agreed to release me.

Listen, just release me. Let me do my thing and let me go on my way.

Yes, Stu, we for sure can do that.

But it never happened. Why? I'll never know. Maybe the Outlaws didn't understand their own league's bylaws. Do I believe it was a cheap shot or spite on Bill's part? No. Unbeknownst to me, and apparently the Outlaws organization, too, at some point I was picked up by the Chicago Blitz and the team never contacted me to claim their property.

The *Star Sports* newspaper headline called my misfortunate a "bureaucratic snafu" in an article that explained the knotty legalese. The news story written by Bob Gretz began, "If you've gone to city hall or the courthouse and stood in line for an hour to renew a license or pay a fee only to learn you are in the wrong line, then you might understand how Stu Crum feels right now."

I had no choice but to leave the Chiefs camp in August of 1984. But that meant I had to sit out the entire NFL season and wait to join the Chicago Blitz when the USFL season began the following spring. By the time flowers began to bloom, the Blitz and the league had folded.

The turn of events meant that by summer of 1985, the rights to kicker Stu Crum reverted to the Jets organization. When I was invited to the club's minicamp, I was in my third year as a professional player. Time was running out on my dream-come-true scenario.

Regardless, I was ready and willing to compete for a place on the Jets' roster, even

though Patrick Leahy, having a great year in a previous season, was kicking well. You might blame the end of my pro career on the rules, bad business models, legal squabbles, or a simple twist of fate. I blame my shoes.

The Jets had an Astroturf practice field for the kickers, as well as a grass field. On the Astroturf field I was flawless during the three-day minicamp. I couldn't miss.

Then the coaches moved the kickers, with snappers and holders, to the grass field. One guy focused on kicking extra points, and another guy kicked from 30 yards. So I said, "Listen, guys, I'm kicking well, so I'll practice at 40 yards out." I thought I was giving everyone the space they needed to concentrate on their form.

On grass I missed at least 50 percent of my kicks because my foot was slipping. I had been planting so hard on Astroturf that I had not figured out my grass plant foot. I looked horrible slipping and sliding. The coaches cut me after minicamp.

Only then, drowning in disappointment, did I realize my mistake. I was still wearing my Astroturf shoes when we shifted to the grass field. I would have avoided the train wreck, and possibly saved my career, if I had thought to change into my grass cleats.

That said, there was one thing I found strange. Joe Pascale was the coach on the field throughout the minicamp. He witnessed my perfection when kicking on Astroturf. I was by far the ace among the kickers. I couldn't miss.

So I called Joe after I was cut and appealed to him. "Coach, you know how good I am."

He just hemmed and hawed, rather than side with me. Was it a grudge?

Nothing personal, I suspect. Football is a business, and three years earlier I had walked away from a Jets contract to become the first player to sign with the Oklahoma Outlaws. So there was no loyalty to me in New York. They had invited me to camp because they owned my rights. There was no obligation to sign me, and I have no hard feelings toward the Jets organization.

My pro career was over.

But a loving, enduring life with Mia was just beginning.

Stu Speak

"Day after day, week after week, we go through the same routine, take care of daily hassles, and before we know it, in a flash, another year has gone by. We didn't make the changes or progress we wanted to make, and so we feel stuck, helpless, and dissatisfied with life."

The Intentional Playbook
Fighting through Adversity

How do you handle difficult times in your life? The way you respond—and the resulting outcome—is within your control.

But we all need support. You are not alone.

Mentally prepare yourself for adversity.
No matter how well you plan ahead, there will always be setbacks and challenges. Confront the situation head-on by deciding whether you will allow your experience to make you or break you. The outcome is dependent upon how you choose to perceive it.

Keep perspective.
Acknowledging and accepting adversity are essential to helping you overcome it. Remind yourself that others have faced similar challenges, that tough times are part of life. And then realign your thinking: ask yourself whether the challenge will be meaningful in three to six months from now. Will it matter to your future self?

DON'T GET TOO HIGH OR TOO LOW.

Achieving that balance is easier said than done—but it's so important to having a healthy outlook. Give yourself a gentle reminder that "life happens," reinforcing that while difficulties will happen, you can control only how you respond to them. Overreacting takes an emotional and physical toll—be disciplined in your thoughts.

TAKE A BREAK.

So often we get consumed by self-doubt, get crippled by problem-solving—the challenge seems too big, too overwhelming. There is benefit to clearing your head: take a physical break (leave your office/home and take a walk), meditate, pray, exercise, listen to music, etc.

FIND THE WHY.

Challenge yourself to find the lesson in the situation. Figure out the "why." Why is this happening to you? Would it have happened if you hadn't taken a certain step that you took? Using a life challenge as an opportunity to learn and grow is a profound way to change the trajectory of a tough situation.

REMIND YOURSELF OF THE GOOD THINGS IN YOUR LIFE.

We all have much to be thankful for—but when we're in the middle of a firestorm, it's difficult to see through to the other side. Perspective is powerful. Write down positive thoughts and daily gratitude or simply focus on those good things: look/scroll through photos, reach out to a friend or family member you haven't talked to in a while—these are simple ways to refocus your energy and attention to the things/people in your life that are most important.

SEEK COUNSEL.

You're not alone! Look for outside guidance: if you're confronting a workplace challenge, talk to a mentor or colleague; if you're facing difficulty in your personal life, connect with a friend, pastor, or counselor. Educate yourself about your options from trusted resources (listen to podcasts, read blogs, books, etc.). And be mindful of the people whom you surround yourself with every day—choose to spend time with those who are a positive influence and who are making choices that align with your values.

I've learned that dealing with challenges is an hour-by-hour, day-by-day exercise.

Some days are easier than others, but I try to start each day with a positive, can-do attitude.

It's not how you start but how you finish.

10

MIA

Now these are Mia's words . . .

Stu has always been about relationships. People matter to him. That's why it was difficult when he had tough decisions to make as a corporate leader. He was not a cool and calculating man. He knew that doing what was right, but not necessarily popular, would have an impact on the men and women he led. That's what I mean when I say I fell in love with his heart. Stu "walked his talk" as a Christian man and leader.

Our first dinner together also revealed Stu's integrity. He didn't intend to woo me. We took off the blinders and began a discussion that was broad and deep. He wasn't interested in hiding anything from me. From the start, he confided in me. That's how I fell in love with his integrity.

Our love story grew, and many whimsical dates followed. I learned that although Stu was driven and determined to succeed, he wasn't rigid or uptight. He liked to laugh and have fun.

Despite all the good I saw in Stu, I was a 21-year-old senior in college who had fallen in love with a *divorced* man I wanted to marry.

It helped that Stu loved my family's European heritage.

My parents came to the United States in 1959 for my father to attend seminary in St. Louis. My father, raised in the Quaker faith, was forced to serve in the German army after being drafted at age 17. He was shot and left to die on the Russian front, but an American soldier saved his life and brought him to an American prisoner of war hospital. It was there that my father had a calling on his life to serve in America. He created innovative social services for poor and marginalized citizens. This example of service was a deep foundation of my upbringing. Stu and I shared similar convictions.

When we sat down together for dinner the first time, good German-style food was served, and music played in the background. Stu told me later that he loved the "feel" of my family home. It was different from most American households, as it expressed a worldly perspective of life. That made me laugh because as a girl we were a bilingual family who spoke German in our home, and I always felt different. I didn't want to be German. I just wanted to be a normal American kid.

After dating for about six months, Stu proposed during a romantic countryside picnic. I was ecstatic. Stu expressed his belief that God had brought us together for life. This began the building of our foundation, the cornerstone being our shared faith in Christ.

We were in love and married in December of 1985. My loving father performed our ceremony and said, "With joy, you may now kiss my daughter." We were husband and wife and started a new chapter together.

Tulsa felt like home to Stu, who had developed strong relationships in the academic, business, and church communities. As he commenced his Texaco career, I continued to serve the population in ways my parents had taught me. Service was a way of life growing up and would continue in the Stu and Mia Crum family.

Early marriage was wonderful and a time for spiritual growth. We dived into activities at our local church and dedicated ourselves to a ministry called Young Life. We also hosted Bible studies in our home and developed life-long friendships.

We would stay in Tulsa for about five years as Texaco placed Stu in various assignments to help him fulfill the potential that corporate leaders had recognized in him from the very start. We left Tulsa when Stu was promoted to regional director in St. Louis. His responsibilities would continue to expand until he became manager of a three-state region.

The new position also meant that we could finally afford to travel. Our first big trip was to Germany, where we explored the region and met my extended family. We didn't realize I was pregnant with our first child until we returned to Tulsa. In our long talks before marriage Stu and I both confessed we wanted children, and "if we could afford it," I would stay at home in the early years with the kids.

When Katherine arrived, Stu and I struggled to get by on one income. We couldn't afford a second car and other amenities, which left me stranded at home for a time. Yet it was the best solution because Stu worked long hours. He would always be home for dinner, so as not to scrimp on time with family. But after he tucked in mom and daughter for a good night's sleep, Stu would return to the office and work until 10:30 p.m. Back then, remote work wasn't possible. Apple, Dell, and Microsoft had not yet invented the personal computer and its operating software.

Six months after Katherine's birth, Stu was promoted to his first management position. He was given a company car and a significant raise. Looking back, it was a bit like ascending a staircase. Our view of the world expanded with each new challenge, which included the arrival of our son, Clayton.

Stu's next assignment took our family of four to Kansas City.

As Stu excelled at Texaco, I was a full-time mom who soon realized I must also fashion my own identity as a not-so-typical corporate wife. It can be daunting to walk into large gatherings where you don't know anyone but your husband. Yet I learned a lot from my mother, Renate's, natural, open-hearted hospitality. She had a gift for starting a conversation with just about anyone, anywhere. I knew I would need those survival skills when Stu, with a big grin, told me we would be flying to New Zealand for a new job interview.

I believe there is something to be said for supporting a spouse and helping him grow simply by being present and pleasant and, in my own way, professional. Not merely to acquire status and material wealth. We were more than corporate climbers and the parents of cute kids who would eventually live in a nice, big house.

In marriage, our bond was our love for each other and faith in God. Through those values, our intention was to create a legacy of giving and contributing to the greater good.

Stu traveled a lot.

I was home with the children. But that, too, was a leadership role.

MIA SPEAK

Women must do what is best for their family. Start a career or stay at home or combine both. In any case, find your worth. Strengthen your faith. Find support. Build a community.

STU SPEAK

No married businessperson can enjoy success without the support of his spouse and children. Mia has not worked outside the home since Katherine was born. I brought in the paychecks, but she is as responsible for my financial success as I am.

THE INTENTIONAL PLAYBOOK
THE 10-SECOND RULE

There was a time in my life when I would speak before I thought, and I didn't realize the consequences of what I was about to say.

Before I left Kansas City for New Zealand in 1994, my boss shared a performance review that included this comment: "Stu, you will have a great future with this company if you learn to think before you speak."

In my mid-30s I finally learned that if I wanted to have a successful career as a leader, foster a successful marriage, become a great father, and be a better friend, I had better learn to think before I spoke.

The 10-Second Rule became a game changer for me, though I had to alter it a bit.

The rule was originally intended to cool down arguments. Whenever the temperature in a conversation starts to rise, pause for 10 seconds before responding.

My problem was not that I said stupid things in a heated conversation but that I said stupid and hurtful things in normal, uncontested social chats. Therefore, whenever I felt on the verge of mouthing off—and being reprimanded by Mia—I would shut up and wait 10 seconds.

The 10-Second Rule works because it allows you to take a moment to consider the person on the other side of the conversation and process whatever it is they just said that may have triggered the need to be flip, defensive, or rudely humorous.

The rule also gave me a moment to ask myself how I would feel if someone else uttered the words that were on the tip of my tongue. A mere 10 seconds gave me time to think rather than react.

Of course, just because it is a simple rule doesn't mean it is easily put into practice.

Emotional reactions are difficult to control.

The 10-Second Rule saved me from saying hurtful things and, to my surprise, also helped a conversation get back on track, whether heated or spiraling out of control.

Ultimately, the real reason for this rule is to remind us that conversation is not just talk. Conversation is meant to create and support relationships. Emotionally intelligent leaders realize this and know when to pause.

Do you find yourself needing to win the conversation?

Explore a new intention, such as adding value, which is difficult to do when you are frustrated, feel angry, or believe you are a stand-up comedian.

I love the 10-Second Rule because I am still married after 39 wonderful years and my grown children still speak to me.

11

GLOBAL CITIZENS

Mia and I took important strides in Tulsa, St. Louis, and Kansas City. Our early years of marriage were a source of joy as we continued to define our marital intentions. When Katherine and Clayton arrived, our responsibilities deepened, and we grew as parents, yes, but also as a loving couple. As we nurtured our children, we remained supportive of each other, which created the foundation that would serve us so well when we moved to Australasia.

The *New Zealand Oxford Dictionary* defines Australasia as several islands—Australia, New Zealand, New Guinea—or only as Australia and New Zealand. In any case, when we moved south of Asia to Auckland, Mia and I could rightfully utter the famous line from *The Wizard of Oz*: "We're not in Kansas anymore."

In other words, we had become global citizens.

The change was at times panoramic, emotionally and intellectually. It felt *big* to be well beyond the US borders and our birth-nation's accepted traditions and beliefs. Also, far, far away from our families and circle of friends.

Yet as we accepted our new identity as Kiwis, or New Zealanders, the change could, at times, feel as intimate as a Polaroid snapshot. As I commenced my duties with an entirely new crew, I quickly learned that people from all walks and territories want the same things:

- Listen to me
- Encourage me
- Give me a chance to succeed
- Show me that leadership has my back

So all the success I had enjoyed as a Yank leading and motivating people at Texaco easily translated to my new surroundings. The company name was Caltex NZ, and at 34 years of age I was responsible for managing retail on the North Island and helping Mia raise our children, Katherine, 4, and Clayton, 2.

As I began to unpack the full range of my leadership skills, I also developed a new appreciation for what it meant to give of myself. Giving requires a certain state of mind and heart, a place much deeper than the material resources a large company can provide. A shift from a *me* orientation to a *we* orientation is essential because it allows a leader to look at people and situations differently. I did not consider what my team could do for me so that I could raise my status within the company. Instead, I focused on what I could do for the individuals I was leading. The mindset shifts from consumption to contribution. Simply put, my devotion to the service leader concept expanded. When you serve, your cup will fill and overflow.

Far from the Tulsa football field where I had learned and experienced so much, I began to acknowledge the fullness of my life, even at a relatively young age. And I understood that service doesn't start when we believe we finally have something to give—incorrectly seeing age and maturity as requirements—but rather it blossoms naturally when we have nothing left to take.

That is a powerful place to be. It happens by becoming conscious of everything we have already received, expressing gratitude, and then intentionally paying it forward with a heart of joy.

"We can do no great things—only small things with great love."
—Mother Teresa

Defining an intention in any phase of life is important because it is not just what we do that matters. It's the inner impetus behind our actions that really counts.

Any time we practice the smallest act of service—even holding a door for somebody—a full heart is asking, "May I be of use to this person?" That kind of giving changes the deeply embedded habit of self-centeredness. In that brief moment, *me* is replaced with *we*.

This is why no true act of service, however small, can ever really be wasted. To serve unconditionally in this way takes a constant effort to remain alert. But with time and sharpened awareness, we begin to brush up against the potential for transformation that is embedded in every act of generosity. The amazing realization is this: when you give, you also receive. The experience is not merely intellectual. You begin to internalize the benefits. Over time, the many acts, those small moments, lead to a different state of being—a state in which service becomes increasingly effortless.

THE EXPAT BENEFITS

I moved up the corporate ladder when I was hired by Caltex, and so most folks back home may have assumed that my pay scale increased. In fact, I accepted a modest raise, because it is not considered a hardship to relocate to New Zealand—a glorious, pristine environment—as opposed to a war-torn area of the world. We were okay with the income because the real benefit of the expatriate experience is not the money but the people and the place.

Toward the end of my original assignment, I was offered a promotion that required us to move again, to Wellington, the capital city of New Zealand, and to some degree start all over making friends and growing acquainted with a new community.

Caltex, an American company that at the time was owned by Chevron and Texaco, naturally had an affiliation with the US Embassy in New Zealand. Mia and I were welcomed into events that allowed us to meet people who brought new perspectives to our lives. Our vision and awareness of the world grew leaps and bounds.

Were Mia and I still proud to be Americans? Absolutely. But we were also enchanted with our global citizenship. It would be the only time our family lived outside of North American borders, even though my corporate responsibilities would take me all over the world.

Another significant factor was our continued commitment to our faith.

When we choose to be in service to others, and the needs of the current situation become clearer, we begin to see new opportunities. When this happens, the giving is not a chore. In fact, it becomes easier, almost effortless, because we become instruments of a greater order. We have created an ecosystem—in business or community life—that has a life of its own, with inherent, intentional plans and strategies.

In New Zealand, Mia and I got involved in extracurricular activities that became our own ecosystem of service leadership. For example, we established a children's ministry at the church we attended.

We also began what we called the $20 ministry. It was spontaneous and direct and required that we both keep cash in our pockets. Sometimes, in the spur of the moment, we discreetly gifted a $20 bill to someone who was needy, hardworking, or we thought might need a little encouragement. If it felt right, we gave.

Was it a grand gesture? No. Did we expect applause? Of course not. Our ministry was intended to be modest and sincere. And while we hoped the recipient would be happy with the money, the gift was a reminder to me and Mia of the vow we had agreed on when we were married:

The money we earn is God given. What flows in must flow out.

STU SPEAK

Be proactive, not reactive. We have all felt the dread that comes from being pressured into giving, such as when friends ask us to donate to their fundraisers. In these cases, we are more likely to give to avoid humiliation rather than out of generosity and concern. This type of giving doesn't lead to a warm-glow feeling; more likely it will lead to resentment. Instead, we should set aside time, think about our options, and find the best charity for our values.

THE INTENTIONAL PLAYBOOK
GENEROSITY

When I die, I want to be known as a person of generosity. **Generosity is a virtue that transcends material wealth and encompasses the essence of true humanity.**

It is not merely about giving away possessions or money but rather about the willingness to share and uplift others through selflessness and compassion. As the saying goes, "Where my treasure is, there lies my heart," indicating that what we hold dear reflects our priorities and values.

In today's world, where individualism often takes precedence, generosity stands out as a beacon of hope and kindness. It is a quality that not only benefits those on the receiving end but also nourishes the giver's soul and fosters a sense of interconnectedness. *When we give generously, we open ourselves up to a profound sense of fulfillment and purpose,* knowing that we have made a positive impact on someone else's life.

Generosity takes many forms, ranging from financial assistance to acts of service and emotional support. It can be as simple as offering a helping hand to a neighbor in need, donating time to a charitable cause, or lending a listening ear to a friend going through a tough time.

The beauty of generosity lies in its simplicity and the potential for creating lasting bonds between individuals. *When we choose to be generous, we experience a shift in perspective.* We start seeing beyond our own needs and desires, becoming aware of the struggles and challenges faced by others. This awareness allows us to empathize and relate to their experiences, fostering a sense of compassion and unity.

Through our generosity, we acknowledge that we are all interconnected, and by helping one another, we create a ripple effect that extends far beyond our immediate circle. Moreover, acts of generosity serve as an inspiration for others to follow suit. When we witness someone selflessly giving their time, resources, or expertise, it ignites a spark within us. It reminds us of the power we possess to make a difference and motivates us to extend a helping hand to those in need. In this way, generosity has the potential to create a cycle of kindness and compassion that spreads throughout our communities and society.

It is important to note that generosity should not be limited to material possessions. While financial contributions are undoubtedly valuable, true generosity goes beyond monetary means. It encompasses our time, skills, knowledge, and, most importantly, our genuine care for others. By giving what we can and sharing our unique gifts, we inspire and empower individuals to unlock their full potential.

A generous leader understands the significance of investing in the growth and development of their team members, valuing diversity, and championing effective communication. Their actions speak louder than words, setting an example for others to follow and creating an environment where individuals can thrive.

Generosity is a powerful force that can transform lives and leave a lasting legacy. By embracing a mindset of abundance and selflessness, we unlock the true potential within ourselves and those around us.

Whether it is through financial contributions, acts of service, or emotional support, generosity has the power to bring about positive change in our communities and society.

As we prioritize generosity and understand that "where our treasure is, there lies our heart," we pave the way for a world that values compassion, kindness, and shared humanity.

12

HOMEWARD BOUND

My first position as the Caltex regional manager of the North Island lasted two years, which we spent in Auckland. I was responsible for 125 convenience store gas stations.

When I was promoted to head of retail for Caltex, we moved south to Wellington and spent two years there as well. The intention of adding an international position to my résumé had worked out well for me, but also Mia, Katherine, and Clayton. And since each assignment had arrived with a well-defined two-year contract, I suppose in the back of our minds we knew our overseas experiment would be tolerable even if things did not go so well.

Then came a surprise offer that forced us to rethink the intentions that had taken us so far from our American roots.

Caltex asked me to join its global operations and marketing team in Singapore. It was another step up in my quest to become a CEO and a position with an assortment of benefits. At that point I was quite sure that the first 20 years of my career would be formative, and each new position was a stepping stone.

Another factor was my firm belief that a CEO is a generalist who must understand the balance sheet, operations, human resources, and—in my industry—the all-important strategy of mergers and acquisitions. Singapore was the epicenter of Caltex's M&A department.

In Singapore I would also oversee a group of companies and provide support for the managers in various nations. In short, the new position gave me the global experience and influence I craved.

Yet the new assignment also included a plot twist and a new measure of commitment.

During my years in New Zealand, I was on loan from Texaco to Caltex. My employment was a joint venture arrangement between Chevron and Texaco. If I accepted the new offer, I would leave the mothership, so to speak, and become a full-time Caltex employee. Not a bad scenario, though I was loyal to Texaco for training me and providing my first taste of upward mobility. Not to mention the company was enormous, with ample opportunities for growth.

The bigger challenge was that Caltex would need us to move to Singapore—indefinitely. In doing so, we would commit to being a full-time expat family because Caltex's operations were global. The only presence they had in North America was a very small operation in Dallas.

Mia and I were faced with a very big decision.

If we accepted the lucrative and attractive position with Caltex, we would spend the next 20 or 30 years working and residing overseas. By the way, there are many Americans who are only too happy to embrace an expat career and lifestyle. It certainly has its attractions.

So the decision was not easy for me, a man who loves to compete and win. And it was not easy for Mia, who is the CEO of our home life and keen on keeping everyone happy.

But after prayerful deliberations, we both agreed that we wanted our children to experience a full American upbringing, including proms and Friday night football games.

More important, we wanted the children to have a relationship with their grandparents. When you're living on the other side of the world, whether it's Singapore, New Zealand, or South Africa—all locations that may have been included in our Caltex tenure—it is naive to think that long trips back home will sufficiently quench the thirst for family. So as much as we relished being global citizens and the enhanced worldview it gave us, we were homeward bound.

Holá, Houston

Intentions sometimes have a funny way of playing out. When we moved back to the States, I was named director of marketing lubes and coolants for Texaco, responsible for Havoline motor oil and many other oil products. As the global brand manager, I traveled to distant foreign ports quite often over the next three to four years.

Was it ironic that I'd turned down the Singapore position so that we could move back to the States only to be rewarded with a different job that provided similar international opportunities? It would be easy to conclude that my faith in God's plan had panned out. But I see it in a different light. Through the years Mia and I have made a lot of tough decisions together. Each time we did what we thought was right, and we never looked back or worried that we might have passed up an important opportunity.

The same was true years before when I developed a personal relationship with Christ. I decided I would not drink alcohol because I didn't like the taste and it made me sick. Little did I know that when I became a businessman my youthful decision would have a social impact. It meant that I would not spend after-hours time carousing and bonding with "the boys."

Did I ever fret that my choice had limited my success in corporate life? No.

in·ten·tion
[in'ten(t)SHen]
NOUN
   1.   a thing intended; an aim or plan

I didn't define my intentions to do me harm. In some cases they were meant to protect me. If I was true to my intentions, the pressure was not on me but on those I worked with. Take me as I am. And they did.

An intention is not handcuffs or a tightrope you must walk. Being clear about who you are—your ambitions and actions—is liberating.

But as we prospered in Houston, circumstances demanded that I clarify my intention even further.

A few years after my global brand role, I was promoted to director of marketing for a downstream joint venture formed by Texaco and Shell. Included in my responsibilities were marketing and advertising in North America for the Shell and Texaco retail brands. Despite the importance of my department's work, I yearned to return to operations, especially after Shell bought Texaco's downstream business—refining and marketing—and I became a Shell employee. Suddenly, there was a dilemma: my colleagues at Texaco were aware of my full background, but the Shell staff knew me only as a director of marketing.

The misperception was at odds with the way I saw myself, which was operational, the kind of guy who leads businesses. I grew concerned that I might be pigeonholed at Shell if I didn't make a change.

After eight years in Houston, an opportunity in Latin America became available, and its broad demands appealed to me. If I could talk my way into the position, I would be running what we called North Latin America, which included Mexico, all of the Caribbean, all of Central America, and northern South America, which consisted of Ecuador, Peru, Colombia, Venezuela, Suriname, Guyana, and French Guyana.

There was just one problem, and it was brought to my attention by the man I had asked to suggest me for the job—my current boss.

"But, Stu, you don't speak Spanish!"

"Boss, I see myself as an operator, not a marketing guy. At least let me interview for the position."

The dilemma felt familiar. When I made a cold call to leadership in New Zealand all those years ago, I was not qualified for the Auckland job. But I pushed for an interview.

Put me in, Coach!

The multilingual man who would make the ultimate decision was Puerto Rican, located in Brazil, and spoke excellent English. He politely mentioned my lack of Español, which he stressed might come in handy operating 1,300 locations in 38 countries throughout Latin America.

But there was a catch. Or an angle I might pursue. Call it wiggle room.

Throughout the region I would operate in, four languages were predominant.

French Guyana speaks *French*.

Suriname speaks *Dutch*.

Columbia, Ecuador, Peru, Costa Rica, and Venezuela all speak *Spanish*.

English anyone? Bahamas, Bermuda, and Belize.

Was I expected to master *three* new tongues?

"I'll learn Spanish," I said. Based on my logic, knowing two of four languages would be sufficient. Then I pressed the issue that was most important. "My background and the *operational* skills I have developed through the years make me a strong candidate for this position. I guarantee no on-the-job training will be necessary."

I never did master Spanish. But I learned enough to be quite effective in restaurants and airports. Fortunately, the members of my leadership team all spoke spotless English and helped me survive and thrive. I could not have known that when I pursued the job. I have witnessed so many small "miracles" through the years as I honed and respected my intentions.

Dare I repeat myself: my intention was to return to operations. Why? To become a CEO I knew I had to prove I could run a business and manage the profit/loss equation. In fact, you are not hired to merely "manage" people and places. You are hired to be a visionary and create profits for the corporation. The Latin America position gave me ample opportunity to thrive or self-destruct. In Miami.

ADIÓS, HOUSTON

My new position was headquartered in Miami. Once again I asked my family to make a sacrifice so that we could prosper in new ways. Thankfully, Mia and I were mindful that we had already accomplished significant intentions by moving back to the United States. Katherine and Clayton, now 14 and 12, had bonded with our extended family and enjoyed the rites of passage as American kids.

Six months later we were back in Houston. *Holá.*

When we moved to the Miami area, Mia and I chose a home in a gated community outside of Miami, Florida. From a logistical standpoint, the location fulfilled our needs. I could get to the office and the airport without much fuss, our children would attend good schools, and I would know everyone was safe while I jetted throughout the Southern Hemisphere. What else could we want?

Shared values.

Several months after arriving, Mia and I disliked the environment, not the sun and fun but the entitlement attitude that was pervasive in our community.

This may sound judgmental. In a sense, it was the opposite. Mia and I were grateful for my new position, but the healthy upbringing of our children was the most important thing in our lives. We made the decision to ask my boss for his blessing to move back to Houston so that we could plug back into their familiar surroundings of church, friends, and community.

"The only thing more dangerous than ignorance is arrogance."
—Albert Einstein

Mia and I talked and prayed, and then I called my boss.

I explained my home life situation, then diplomatically announced that one of two things must happen. Either allow me to move back to Houston or I must leave the company.

Does that sound like an arrogant demand? I made concessions that I hoped would soften the blow and keep me in the job that I enjoyed so much:

- I keep Miami as my headquarters and work from that office as required. (Truthfully, I was rarely in the Magic City since I traveled so much.)
- I pay for all new travel expenses resulting from my move to Texas.
- I pay all relocation costs.
- I pay for a new home.

The expenses I list are normally covered by the employer.

Money was not the only factor.

The move to Houston would add more flying time to my already frenzied schedule. Of the 52 weeks on the calendar, 48 would be for travel. Basically, I was in a different country every week, always on the move. I rarely saw my office in Miami, where my support staff was located, or my home in Houston (we moved back to the same neighborhood so that friendships and our church association could resume). Had we thought of it, the Crum family might have invented its own board game called *Where's Stu Now?*

Typically, El Salvador, Guatemala, Bermuda, Venezuela, or Colombia.

My boss kindly agreed to my requests.

All things must pass. Three years later I was named vice president of sales in the lubricants division. From there I moved to president of Jiffy Lube.

Much to my surprise, when I left the Latin America assignment, the company reimbursed me for all those extra expenses I had paid. Apparently, by taking a new position that kept me in Houston, Shell saved a lot of money on relocation costs. To this day we know this was one of the most important parenting decisions we ever made.

Stu Speak

Success can become a heady experience. Flying all over the world, engaging with gifted and celebrated people—how do you keep an even keel? I start with the basic things to be thankful for on this day or any day. I am thankful for each breath I take. I am thankful for each sip of water. I am thankful for food—and my health. I am thankful for the people in my life who care about me. Yes, I've been fortunate throughout my career. But not without a lot of team spirit along the way and the reminder of simple, humbling pleasures.

THE INTENTIONAL PLAYBOOK
WINNING AND LEADERSHIP COME AT A PRICE

If you want to pursue success and win and if you want to be a great leader, these intentions come at a price.

Winning is often accompanied by visions of triumph, achievement, and the satisfaction of reaching a goal. **But behind every victory we also find dedication, perseverance, and sacrifice.**

Winning requires a commitment to excellence and an unwavering desire to succeed. **It demands countless hours of hard work, discipline, and self-improvement.** It necessitates pushing ourselves beyond our limits and constantly challenging the status quo.

The price of winning extends beyond physical exertion; it also encompasses mental and emotional strain.

The fear of failure, the pressure to perform, and the weight of expectations can take a toll on one's well-being.

Sacrifice. Is it in you? Can you forgo leisure time, social activities, etc.? Winning demands a diet of short-term sacrifices for long-term gains. It requires prioritizing goals and making tough choices. Leadership comes with immense responsibilities and expectations. We must be role models and set high standards. **This level of accountability can be daunting and overwhelming.**

Leadership demands vision, courage, and **the ability to navigate through uncertainty.** It means taking responsibility for both successes and failures and being accountable for the consequences of one's actions.

Leaders may have to make unpopular decisions or face criticism and resistance from those who do not share their vision. Being a leader means shouldering the weight of the entire team and ensuring their well-being and growth.

Furthermore, leaders often have to sacrifice personal ambitions for the collective good. They must prioritize the needs of their team over their own desires. This sacrifice can be in the form of time, resources, or even personal aspirations. Leadership demands selflessness.

Ultimately, the rewards that come with winning and effective leadership far outweigh the costs. The lessons learned, the personal growth achieved, and the impact made on others are invaluable.

True success is measured not only by the end results but also by the journey, sacrifices, and growth we endure along the way.

Ask yourself the hard question: is it in you?

13

BODYGUARDS AND DISNEYLAND

If my Latin America tenure demanded that I travel a lot, that did not mean I never saw my family. My vision of excelling as a corporate leader was always paired with my dedication to being a good father and husband. My kids needed and deserved two parents, not just one—Mia, chief operating officer of our Houston homestead and love of my life.

To achieve harmony, on Monday I was on an airplane heading to my headquarters in Miami or destinations in Central and South America. On Thursday I was on a flight home. This meant I was with my family from Thursday evening through Monday morning. And since I took seriously Lee Iacocca's admonition that a man cannot be a great father and a great golfer at the same time, I was always present and accounted for when in Houston. Who wouldn't want to be? It was fun.

Yes, there are sacrifices. I didn't always love boarding an aircraft after enjoying a weekend at home. Nor was I a supreme being who could call his own shots at every turn of the road. There were disruptions and surprises, and I worked for an expansive corporation that had huge expectations. I did my best to balance it all by being very clear about my own intentions—professional and personal. My favorite word and guiding light gained new significance on my first travel assignment in Latin America.

Boutique Bodyguards

It was intimidating in the beginning, for sure. On my first trip, I walked off the plane, and the country manager greeted me and then introduce me to his bodyguard.

Yes, *bodyguard*.

I found it extremely humbling. Perhaps because the first response is physical, a hint of fear trembling in your bones. Then it is disbelief. You mean I am not free to roam about the country?

Maybe surprise was all I was experiencing. While I interviewed for the position, no one ever mentioned that kidnapping was a boutique business in some parts of my new region of responsibility—including Colombia, El Salvador, Guatemala, Nicaragua, Honduras, and Venezuela.

The leaders of those markets, who lived there full time, had full-time bodyguards who accompanied us everywhere and served as drivers. They were armed and capable chauffeurs who were hired to protect us. I soon learned that to help them do their job, I must never wear branded clothing that shouts, "This guy is an American who works for a rich international corporation."

In Colombia, the leader of that market told me about the time his family member was kidnapped.

"What do you mean it's a boutique business?" I asked.

"When they kidnap you, they don't want to kill you."

"That's refreshing."

"But they want money."

"Lots of money."

He smiled. "Si, señor."

"They kidnap you to extort money."

"Ransom, yes. That's why we never wear anything that has the Shell company logo, because if you wore brands that told the potential kidnappers that, hey, this is a big-oil person, they have money—"

"You become a target."

From the time I landed in the country to the time I left the country, I had driver-bodyguards. They accompanied me when I visited my convenience stores and gas stations and when we went to lunch or dinner. They also walked me into my hotel at the end of the day and escorted me out of the lobby into a car when my day began. They were with me the entire time I was in public.

It did not take long to become friends with the men who protected me and to accept the necessary precautions. Yet the experience also made me ponder my start with Texaco. The managers I met in various countries were performing the same types of duties as I did in Kansas City. What if I had needed "muscle" in those days? And Mia, too (because the spouses of the senior-level Latin American employees were also provided bodyguards)?

The protection did not end for these leaders after their workday. Bodyguards would drive them home to armed gated communities. You didn't just tap in a code to open the entrance at these locations. The security was essential for everyone who lived in that community, but not everyone had bodyguards.

Our senior-level officials in these nations also employed full-time in-house help who cooked meals, did the laundry, and kept the homes spick-and-span. These men earned less income than me but could afford the assistance because the cost of living was so low in many of these countries. At the time, I still mowed my own lawn and did much of the yard work.

When Mia visited me, we would marvel that we would not need the bodyguard protection if we were mere tourists. But I was representing Shell, and the company needed to protect employees and their brand.

These were some of the most enjoyable years of my career. The people and the teammates in Latin America were some of the most welcoming, caring, family-oriented people I have ever worked with in my life. They were very educated, cultured, and multilingual—and wow could they dance.

INTENTIONAL TRAVEL

My children certainly didn't understand the dangers and complexities of my extensive travels. And in some ways, they were still too young to fully appreciate our ability as a family to spend time together in foreign lands. The vacations and travel were often strategic and therefore intentional.

We spent a lovely Thanksgiving in Costa Rica. We spent another wonderful spring break in the Bahamas.

Even before my three-plus years in Latin America, family travel was on the agenda. When I was director of Shell's global marketing department, Katherine and Clayton were only 10 and 12, so we chose locations that were fun and suitable for children, like Disneyland—in Tokyo.

From Japan we traveled to Singapore for a few days before landing in Kuala Lumpur, Malaysia, where I had business. While I worked, Mia and the children explored. Once again, spring break was in our favor.

Mia and I had common goals: We wanted our children to understand other cultures and learn from them. We also wanted our children to have a wider view of the world.

One of my marketing roles put me in London, where Royal Dutch Shell was headquartered, four times a year. Occasionally, I would bring the whole family and let them play while I worked, then I would take vacation time so that we could extend the trip and take the high-speed Eurostar train to Paris, a fun way to glide from one great city to another.

I recognize that Mia and I were fortunate to be able to see so much of the world. And I hope my children will do the same for their kids. Not every family can make the same types of travel plans, but that does not mean that moms and dads can't be more intentional about how they share their work demands with family. Sometimes just a visit to your place of work is a world of wonder for a child.

Or think about what simple gifts you can bring home from your road trips, even if you are only crossing state lines, from Oklahoma to Missouri, for example. Mementos, clothing, decals, maps, or whatever else distinguishes your destination from home. Small things may personalize the traveling that takes you away from family while also reminding your spouse and kids that wherever you go, you take them with you—even if in spirit only. There was not a night when I was on the road that I didn't call home to tell my wife and children that I loved them. Never.

Lee Iacocca's wisdom about golf made sense to me because that type of outing with a group or even a couple friends can eat up at least half a day on weekends.

Yet a tennis match early Saturday morning in Houston took less than two hours. It also fulfilled my intense lifelong love of playing to win.

In my world, intentions and fulfillment are the best of friends.

STU SPEAK

Fathers play a crucial and irreplaceable role in the world. Our presence, guidance, and love have a profound impact on the development and well-being of our children. One of the primary roles we play is to provide emotional support and stability for our children. We should be seen as the pillars of strength in our families, offering a sense of security and protection. Research shows that children with involved fathers are more likely to have higher self-esteem, better behavioral outcomes, and healthier relationships throughout their lives.

THE INTENTIONAL PLAYBOOK
I DON'T HAVE ENOUGH TIME AND MONEY!
REALLY?

In today's fast-paced and materialistic world, it is common to hear people complain about a lack of time and money. Many of us feel like we are constantly running on a treadmill, struggling to keep up with our financial responsibilities and daily obligations.

But what if I told you that by prioritizing better, we can have plenty of both?

One of the main reasons people feel like they don't have enough money or time is because they prioritize the wrong things. In our consumer-driven society, we often equate success and happiness with material possessions and wealth. As a result, we spend a significant amount of our time and energy chasing after money, even at the expense of our personal relationships and overall well-being.

Here is the truth: research has shown that there is a diminishing return when it comes to the relationship between money and happiness.

While having enough money to meet our basic needs and live comfortably is important, obsessively pursuing wealth beyond that point does not necessarily lead to greater happiness or fulfillment.

On the other hand, time is a finite resource that we cannot multiply. Every second that passes is gone forever, and once we realize this, we start to understand the value of time. Time is the ultimate currency, and how we choose to spend it reflects our priorities and values.

So how can we prioritize better and ensure that we have plenty of both money and time?

It starts with a shift in mindset and a reevaluation of our values. Instead of solely focusing on accumulating wealth, we should strive to find a balance between work, leisure, and meaningful relationships.

- **Set clear goals and priorities:** Reflect on what truly matters to you and what brings you joy and fulfillment, then write it down. Return to this list. Read it often. It will help you to pursue your passions and true interests. Does this seem obvious? Yet so many people I know ignore it. When you identify your priorities, it becomes easier to allocate your prime resources, money and time.

- **Prioritize:** Learn to say no. We often feel obligated to say yes to every request or opportunity that comes our way, fearing that we might miss out on something important. But saying yes to everything can lead to overcommitment and a lack of balance in our lives. By setting boundaries and learning to say no when necessary, we create more space for the things that truly matter to us.

- **Don't compare:** Avoid falling into the comparison trap. It's crucial. In the age of social media, it is easy to feel inadequate or even lazy or incompetent. Remember that everyone's journey is unique. What works for a colleague may not work for you. Drop the comparison cycle and focus on you—your goals, your values. Then prioritize time and money accordingly.

Prioritizing better can help us have plenty of both money and time. By shifting our mindset, setting clear goals and boundaries, and avoiding comparison, we can create a balanced and fulfilling life. Remember, time is a precious resource, and how we choose to spend it ultimately determines our happiness and well-being. So let's make conscious choices and prioritize what truly matters, ensuring that we have an abundance of both money and time in our lives.

14

OUR CANCER JOURNEY

The year 2007 was a time of great busyness. My daughter, Katherine, was a senior in high school, and naturally we were very involved in her activities. There was so much to do, including visiting colleges she might want to attend the next year.

Mia shared with me that she felt a lump in her breast and a few days later confirmed our greatest fear.

Doctors confirmed that Mia had Stage 2 invasive ductal carcinoma, and it had spread to two lymph nodes. She was looking at surgery, six months of chemotherapy, and radiation. Breast cancer rocked our world. My wife was 42 years old with no breast cancer in her family history.

Her entire life was focused on being Supermom and volunteering throughout our Houston community. Giving support to others had become her forte, her trademark, and now she had to surrender to another reality that allowed people to be there for her.

She didn't like switching roles but found the courage to walk this road with strength and faith.

As it turned out, her journey changed our family for the better.

Cancer made us stronger.

Cancer strengthened our marriage.

Cancer strengthened our faith.

And cancer taught us all that each day is a gift.

I found such beauty in her strength. Her hair fell out. She had numerous side effects but continued to fight this battle.

I was still building a career, needing to travel, but my wife's diagnosis forced me to slow down and be a rock for her. What mattered was beating cancer, and we all fought hard. I tried to make her feel loved and cared for on days when the tears would not stop. I did this with three little words.

"You are beautiful."

STOP SIGN

In some ways, cancer is a stop sign. It tells you that all your expectations and busy habits must change. At least for a while.

It didn't end my business responsibilities, but it forced us to reflect on our choices and pace.

About six months into her treatment, the 2007 holiday season rolled around, but cancer doesn't pause for ceremony. She had a Christmas Eve chemotherapy session scheduled, and the regimen cannot be changed for mere inconvenience.

At 6 p.m. on Christmas Eve, we arrived at the hospital with our children in tow. We came up with the idea to use the occasion as an excuse to spread a little good cheer. Mia wore a big reindeer headband with little bells that dangled, jingled, and jangled in all directions. I was also armed with a basket full of candy canes, which the children and I passed out to all the other patients and their companions.

As a family we wore Santa hats and brought an array of simple gifts. Together we spread out in the waiting room, a candy cane calvary intending to sweeten the day.

But we soon realized that many people were not as fortunate. We were surrounded by unspeakable suffering.

I put a candy cane in the frail hand of a man or woman knowing they probably wouldn't see the next Christmas or bother with New Year's resolutions.

Other patients hunched over in their wheelchairs, attached to an IV, may have been mere steps away from saying goodbye to family and friends.

It was a humbling wake-up call for all of us. We felt hollow for referring to her cancer experience as "a journey" that she would endure and then leave behind, like a discarded cocoon. As awful as she felt after each treatment, we believed that she would be healed and fly from the trauma with the wings of a beautiful butterfly. A different type of storybook ending awaited many of the people who smiled when I handed them candy.

The health scare made us appreciate Mia for all the things she did that we just didn't realize she was doing for us. And we came to realize how precious good health is. It's part of her story, and it's part of our family's story and something that I don't want to call a blessing because blessing wouldn't be the right word. But we grew from this, and from that time onward, Mia has had a ministry working with other women who often are afraid of getting a mammogram.

After that year of treatment, she traveled with me to conferences where she told her story. When I joined Bridgestone, Mia created sessions called Think Pink and Feel Beautiful. She invited doctors to speak about the importance of early detection and mammograms. Her volunteer work has helped hundreds of women endure breast cancer and the emotional aspects of losing hair and undergoing treatment—and daring to dream about the future.

After one of our Think Pink and Feel Beautiful sessions, one of the women who attended came up to Mia and said, "Because you did this today, I will now go get a mammogram."

She once sat with a woman in a waiting room who confessed, "We have no insurance, no health insurance. We've had to mortgage our home because I want to live."

I was so thankful to be an employee of Shell, which offered amazing benefits and health coverage for my beautiful wife.

After a difficult year, Mia rang the bell and was cancer free.

This is the poem she wrote to thank others who helped her on her journey:

> It's hard to know just where to start, what thoughts to share, what words impart.
>
> For here I sit, the journey through and slowly look back at the view.
>
> To think a year has come and gone, so much I've learned, I stand here strong.
>
> The "cancer" word brought fear and doubt, but now with thanks I look about.
>
> I see a woman changed within, a fighting spirit with tougher skin.
>
> A life that's grown from letting go, to walk in faith, and take it slow.
>
> A time to learn and finally see my outward looks won't define me.
>
> But a heart and soul and faith within, that's all that matters in the end.

How can this road be one of strife when it has given me new life?

My view has changed of what is real, how deep to love and how to feel.

Friends and family far and near, I cherish more and hold so dear.

Worries once I thought were grand, I place them now into God's hand.

Each one His hands to slowly sift, for now I know each day's a gift.

The steps I've walked, all new to me, have formed a path that sets me free.

No more are days of fear or dread for now with hope I look ahead.

And wait with joy for what I'll see in all that God has planned for me.

My loving Dad who shared his heart gave words of wisdom from the start.

"Hope keeps you joyful," he'd sweetly say. Those words I cherish to this day.

My Hope does come from God above, I praise Him daily for His love,

And share my road with each of you and for the world to see and view.

For when the journey seems too long, when life is hard, or something's wrong,

There is a place to take our fears, to find sweet rest to wipe our tears.

In Christ I've found this "hiding place" to find the strength each day to face.

His words of HOPE on which I stand, I rest my worries in His hands.

The cancer road that I have walked at first I thought my world it rocked.

But now with grace I say with glee, this caner road has set me free.

I'm free to walk in faith each day, to share in JOY along the way.

Because I know God healed my life, I'm a better mom, a better wife.

A stronger friend, a purer soul, a happier person, I feel more whole.

The cancer road now takes a turn. A "survivor's" life is what I'll learn.

I'll hold with me the blessings true, the love received from all of you.

The journey walked along this road was helped by you who shared my load.

With humble heart and thanks I say, you helped me make it to this day.

You touched my life and all should know.

Praise God from whom all BLESSINGS FLOW!!!!

STU SPEAK

We can't control all our health issues, but we can control attitude. Luck has nothing to do with it. All the unexpected events that come your way are not 'bad luck.' It's just life. Regardless of what is happening in your life right now, you have the power to change your attitude toward it. It may take days, weeks, months, or years. But for sure the one thing it will not take is 'good luck.'

THE INTENTIONAL PLAYBOOK
BE LOVE

Being intentional helps build character by clearing our heads and developing habits that cut through distractions. We take aim and discover that we can fulfill goals that were once just the stuff of dreams.

But intentions do not make us God.

I know it is corny, but every spring when flowers punch up through the soil after a long winter, I think, "That's love."

We can't be God, but we can be love. Cultivate it.

When you feel **helpless**, be love.

When you feel **defeated**, be love.

When you are speechless as you watch others **suffer**, be love.

THREE

LATE-GAME SCORE

15

PEP BOYS AND CARL ICAHN

If the deal to buy Pep Boys had gone through, I never could have left Bridgestone in 2016 after nearly four years as president of retail operations. The deal would have brought 600 new stores into our network and added another $600 million to our revenue. I would not have shirked that responsibility.

A fair question might be, why leave at all? You had launched your Vision 2020 plan and created a new leadership team. Together you had substantially expanded Bridgestone's profit margin and overcome whatever anxieties you felt when you retired from Shell at 53 years young in 2013 after Mia had concluded her post-cancer five-year regimen.

There were reasons, but my departure had nothing to do with the billionaire activist investor Carl Icahn barging in with a bigger bid to acquire Pep Boys.

Our success at Bridgestone came after we put a playbook in place. Our intention was to grow. But at 2,200 stores, how could we expand to 3,000 stores or more? The answer: buy an existing company.

Pep Boys, founded in 1921 and headquartered in Philadelphia, was struggling and looking for a buyer. We began negotiation, came to a purchase and sale agreement, and signed a letter of intent.

Our team flew to the City of Brotherly Love with our CEO to do a town hall-style meetup with 650 Pep Boys employees. A little reassurance never hurts, so we introduced ourselves by saying how excited we were about the deal. Our presentation was well received, and our integration team began their process as we pushed ahead to finalize the agreement. What could go wrong?

Let the bidding wars begin.

A week after our Philadelphia visit, Carl Icahn, a raider well known for disruption, stepped in and said, "I want to buy that business." He made a handsome offer of $16.50 a share in cash after Pep Boys leadership had accepted $15.50 per share in cash from Bridgestone. Things heated up.

We countered Icahn's offer; he countered ours. We were making headlines in major business and news publications—*Carl Icahn Raises Offer for Pep Boys*—but could we make history?

Was the negotiation only about a dollar amount?

Not exactly. Before the finale, I had numerous phone conversations with Icahn. Our talks were amicable, not contentious. We were trying to figure out how to share Pep Boys: Bridgestone wanted to rebrand only the shops where we could replicate our Vision 2020 customer service success. But the nearly 100-year-old enterprise also sold car parts. Would Icahn Enterprises be content to take over that stream of revenue since that type of business was already in its portfolio?

Here's how it was intended to work: Bridgestone would operate repairs in the back of the shops. But when we needed parts—brakes, brake pads, whatever—our servicepeople would walk to the front of the shop, which Carl would own, and buy those parts. A smooth transaction.

Over three months or so, we got close several times. The last interactions happened just before Christmas 2015. The season usually allowed us to relax and take some time off. Not that year. On the verge of a handshake, Icahn tried (not for the first time) to retrade the deal, meaning he had accepted the terms of our agreement then at the last moment tried to negotiate for even better terms.

Finally, the Bridgestone leadership team concluded that an agreement with Icahn Enterprises was out of reach. Instead, we began negotiating with Advance Auto Parts and O'Reilly's to sell them the car parts division of Pep Boys if we could somehow seal a deal with the successors of Manny, Moe, and Jack—the World War I veterans who had founded the business a century before.

No go. Pep Boys accepted Icahn's significantly higher offer that Bridgestone was not inclined to top.

In a press release Pep Boys defined the terms: an all-cash transaction for $18.50 per share. Equity value came to about $1.03 billion. The merger with Icahn Enterprises meant Pep Boys common stock would be removed from listings on the New York Stock Exchange.

A fair question might be, did the Pep Boys drama end your time with Bridgestone? No. Nothing about the negotiations was personal. As the saying goes, "It's just business."

In fact, I loved working for Bridgestone. I consider it my favorite job in an enormously satisfying career. The opportunities were plentiful, and it was thrilling to take part in the transformation of Bridgestone's business culture.

Even negotiating with Carl Icahn was a highlight. He is a rare figure in global finance. Those experiences allowed me to reflect on my trajectory, from a young man determined to be a college and professional athlete to a husband and father who had learned the art of negotiation.

Nonetheless, the Pep Boys events did mark a turning point for me.

Service King Collision Center

Through the years I occasionally took calls from headhunters probing my interest in new job opportunities. So it was not unusual to be contacted by the headhunter of a company called Service King Collision Center.

Let's review. I'd been in management positions and marketing positions, and in Latin America I played a key role in operations, my true love. The big changes in my life often happened because I saw something I wanted or needed—international experience in New Zealand, for example—and I went after it. But all these assignments were with publicly traded corporations.

One area I had not yet explored was private equity, although when the Service King headhunter called, I was sitting on the board of DRB Systems, a company owned by private equity firm Prairie Capital.

Bridgestone had grown at an impressive pace. But the cycles of finance and nature made me wonder whether we could sustain the growth. This fact of life may have caused me to develop an appetite for new horizons.

Bridgestone had treated me very well financially. The salary and bonus structure—in fact, the entire compensation package—was very fair. I'd provided an excellent quality of life for my family, and now my children were out of college and beginning families of their own. I had gladly paid for Katherine's university education (Clayton went to college on a baseball scholarship) and a couple weddings and had stayed at Shell to maintain health care for Mia's travail with cancer. Now I could speculate and take on more financial risk than I had in prior years.

And truth be told, I was like many other men and women in leadership. If I helped improve a business by millions of dollars, that was an exciting challenge. Since my employer was a publicly traded Japanese-owned company, I did not hold stock, nor could I ever expect to have a piece of the prize—equity in the business.

Compare that with a position in a private equity-backed company at a senior level. Under those circumstances, I would be expected to help grow the firm, of course, but I would also be given a piece of the spoils. I would no longer be a mere employee. I would be creating value, for the company and my family.

Intentions. Can they change? Can you suddenly feel a shift in the foundation that has guided and supported your growth for so many years?

"Why?" Mia asked.

"Bigger rewards for the skills I've developed through the years."

"Were there other opportunities you wanted when I had cancer?"

"No. I just wanted you to get well."

"But you're president now. This new position would drop you down a notch, wouldn't it? How is that better for you?"

Mia had made a good point.

The position offered by Service King was COO (chief operating officer), not CEO (chief executive officer). Service King's CEO had been with the company for 25 years and would remain until we sold the business within a couple years. At that time, he would step down, and I would step in as CEO.

"Deferred gratification," Mia said.

I laughed.

"Now I get it."

Once again, Mia and I had made an important decision together. My new intention was to earn a big piece of equity, more money than I had ever made in a short couple of years.

If all went well.

If.

Every intention comes with risks. Usually because intentions ask us to improve or reinvent some aspect of our lives. There are no guarantees. Perhaps I should have given more thought to the company name, which included the word *collision.*

I flew to New York City and interviewed with Blackstone employees, who were also Service King board members. A year and a half later I was not entirely pleased with the path we were on. By then I'd had plenty of time to take a tour of the business, so to speak, just as I had after being hired by Bridgestone. After all, I was not hired to merely watch. And when you want to sell a home and want to get the best price, do you upgrade where you can? Of course. And there was room for improvement at Service King.

Unfortunately, the changes I wanted to make were not embraced by the CEO. His words still sting: *Stu, you just don't understand; we don't do things this way.*

The next meeting was worse. The CEO and head of human resources confronted me and announced, *Stu, your position is not needed.*

When I was hired by Bridgestone, I was told that big changes needed to happen and I would have the full support of the company. At Service King, we all knew that operational advances would raise our valuation, and yet I was being told to leave.

If I was devastated, I could also guess what had precipitated the decision.

Months earlier I met with the CEO for a frank chat. I said, "It doesn't look like the company is going to be sold anytime soon, so it may be time to move on if your job will not be available anytime soon."

THE INTENTIONAL PLAYBOOK FOR SUCCESS IN FAITH, FAMILY, AND BUSINESS | 133

He knew this was the original game plan. He also knew that I had not left a great job so that I could be second in command. So I wasn't pushing him but rather reminding him of the conversations we had during the interview process. If he had merely said, "No, Stu, I'm staying," I would have remained in my position as I looked for a new opportunity.

Blackstone owned Service King, and I had made friends with a couple men who left that company for other private equity firms. Eventually, when some time had passed, I just had to ask, "Why didn't the board step in to nudge our plan forward?"

Both men gave the same answer: it was the CEO's company to run, and they were not going to intervene.

There was another issue at play. I was a highly compensated executive who apparently was not going to ascend to the top spot. Board members may have reasoned that if I was not going to become CEO and the business wasn't changing hands anytime soon, we can save some good money by removing some costs—my compensation package—from the bottom line.

The CEO didn't last long. He was finally fired and replaced. Then three years after my departure, the company failed, went bankrupt, and not a single person walked away with any equity.

A blessing in disguise?

At the time I didn't see it that way. The dismissal of my ideas, and me as a person, really hurt. I took it hard. The pain I experienced reminded me of my senior year in high school when I was cut from the basketball team. Even a grown man who has a lot to be grateful for can suffer disappointment.

For the first time in 33 years or so, I was unemployed. I played a hundred rounds of golf that year working through my feelings. Did my dismissal mean I was not needed anymore or was of no use to anyone? That thought was a body blow.

Fortunately, unemployment allowed Mia and me to travel and spend more time together. If I was dashing to an airport, this time my beautiful wife was right there with me. That was a blessing. Another blessing was about to show itself.

Clayton was not himself. Our beautiful boy was in serious trouble. He needed his family.

He needed me, his dad, and suddenly I had lots of time on my hands.

STU SPEAK

In life, we come across situations that are out of our control. Setbacks, unforeseen circumstances, or external factors disrupt our plans. These situations can make us feel overwhelmed and even powerless. However, amid the chaos, there is one fundamental principle that remains constant: we can only control the controllables.

THE INTENTIONAL PLAYBOOK
IS LESS REALLY MORE?

Our world is fast paced. No wonder the concept of "less is more" is becoming increasingly important. Feeling overwhelmed by a never-ending stream of requests and project demands?

THE "JUST SAY NO!" BENEFITS:

- You prioritize resources and focus on what truly matters. (Yes, you *must* decide what truly matters. Reassess your intentions.)

- You allocate time and energy strategically.

- You dedicate yourself to meaningful activities. This results in greater productivity and success.

- You enjoy improved clarity, direction, and purpose. (Always saying "yes" dilutes the quality of life itself.)

- You create boundaries and maintain a healthy work-life harmony. (Balance? Is there any such thing?)

- You divest of harmful expectations. Available 24/7? Say no and prevent burnout.

- You align with your true values. Excessive workloads or commitments disappear. Overall happiness and satisfaction naturally emerge.

- You embrace trust-based relationships.

16

TRANSPARENCY

During his junior year in high school, my son, Clayton, started getting a lot of attention from colleges and Major League Baseball teams. In a showcase tournament for his age group, his fastball was clocked at 93 miles per hour. He was 17 years old.

The summer before his senior year, Clayton accepted a full-ride scholarship to play baseball at Ohio State University. The opportunity was offered even though he faced Tommy John surgery, an ulnar collateral ligament (UCL) reconstruction of the elbow.

Why would the OSU coaches extend a scholarship before the medical procedure? They knew young athletes could recover from the ordeal.

Clayton did recover and had an exceptional season and was drafted by the Chicago Cubs.

Meanwhile, our attraction to Ohio State changed when the coach who had made the offer to Clayton retired. This was a disappointment because we believed his mentoring would benefit our son. Ohio State kindly released him from his scholarship agreement, and then Clayton accepted a baseball scholarship to the University of Texas.

At the end of his freshman season at Texas, Clayton tweaked his elbow injury and required another surgery—his second.

While in recovery, we decided Texas wasn't the best program for him, so Clayton enrolled at a junior college and was drafted for a second time by the Chicago Cubs. Twice he chose not to sign with the team because he wanted to get a college degree, just like his parents had done.

Instead, he accepted a scholarship to the University of Oregon and pitched his junior year, and months later the Tampa Bay Rays offered a contract and Clayton signed. By then he was a junior at Oregon and started playing professional baseball in the minor leagues.

His first season was terrific, and he was invited to the instructional league, which is a big deal for rookies. The opportunity extends the playing season, where Clayton pitched really well.

It broke our hearts when he returned for his second year as a pro and injured his throwing arm for the third time. Not his elbow but his shoulder, a rotator cuff problem.

A third surgery meant more painkillers. Opioids. Until then, Clayton had avoided any long-term dependence on the drugs. Then a fourth surgery was needed, and our son began to change.

CLAYTON

I soon realized my son struggled finding his identity outside of baseball. I realized that he had become addicted to the painkillers prescribed after his baseball injuries and subsequent surgeries.

We soon realized his abuse of opioids, specifically oxycodone, was an everyday occurrence. That's when his addiction began to spiral and take over his body.

I struggled. My son, an addict? I wondered what I had done wrong.

Nothing.

So many parents feel hopeless when a child turns to drugs. What Mia and I learned is that addiction is not a moral failure. Addiction is a disease. It does not discriminate. It is an equal-opportunity offender.

ROCK BOTTOM

Soon our son hit rock bottom for the last time. As a family we had an intervention and got him the help he needed.

Clayton's confession was devastating to the family. We are a Christian family who see ourselves as an upright family in the community, but now we've got a son who's an addict?

It was more my issue than Mia's. She was more pragmatic and realistic. She could grasp that addiction was not a social label or an indication of social status. It was no different from having cancer or diabetes or some other illness.

In some ways, my reaction to my son's troubles reminded me of my divorce from my first wife. I sought perfection—perfect marriage, perfect family—and anything less felt like an embarrassing failure for a man of faith. Would I now be defined as the father of an addict? And if so, would that embarrass me?

I knew something was wrong when I saw Clayton's behavior go off the rails, but maybe I couldn't admit it, or at least could not fully come to terms with it. The reality was potentially destructive to my pride. Some days I wondered whether I was in as much denial as he was.

The events made me look within. I had to admit that I judged people who had succumbed to drugs as too weak to beat the temptation. After some self-analysis, I was finally able to accept that my son had an issue, yes, but I loved him unconditionally and I was willing to support him through the fight for his life and marriage. I would do it all by putting my ego aside and admitting that addiction could happen to anybody. As a family, we began to work through it.

I drove Clayton to St. Louis, where he began a six-week rehab program recommended by his uncle Rick who had a PhD and studied addiction. Coincidentally, it was the first time in 35 years that I was between jobs. My focus was exactly where it needed to be.

Many addicts relapse multiple times before they get clean. To his credit, Clayton worked hard. Like when he was an MLB prospect. He didn't let up and has not had a relapse. To this day he has mentored more than 100 people who need help overcoming addiction. I am a proud father.

STU SPEAK

Clayton beat his addiction, but he still has an addictive personality. To succeed he turned his addiction to drugs into a fitness regime. When he goes through times of stress and anxiety, he doesn't pop a pill or pour himself a drink. He goes to the gym. Survival is adaptation, in business, family, and faith.

THE INTENTIONAL PLAYBOOK
PRINCIPLE VS. LOVE

My Christian faith taught me the principles of being an upright man. I followed Christ's example as best I could, even while reminding my buddies, "I'm no choir boy." I have moods. I react. I make mistakes.

Love of family has taught me about the paradox of principles. Walking a straight line is not so easy when reality blocks your path.

Clayton's addiction forced me to rethink some assumptions about good and bad and learn evermore the power of forgiveness.

Intentions. Can you put yourself on the other side of your learned or chosen opinions? In other words, can you take the opposite point of view with the intention of learning from it?

Clayton didn't try to convince us that his addiction was a good thing. He didn't try to convert family and friends. He was willing to seek help so that he could change a damaging habit.

Intentions. Hey, Stu, what damaging habits can you change? Can you be as strong as your son, Clayton, was in the face of ruination?

17

A Promise Kept

Once Clayton was on a path to recovery, I was still an unemployed business executive playing a lot of golf. My long walks to the green gave me plenty of time to ponder what my next steps might be.

Although my résumé would speak to my long experience in the automotive sector, in truth the key theme and passion of my previous 20 years of my business life were about change management and creating a new vision for established companies. Those interests fit right in with my newborn intention. The one I would hum, breathe, and pray on as I stared down a fairway or lined up a putt:

I am an entrepreneur who seeks private equity opportunities.

In the fall of 2018 my phone rang. It was a founder of DRB Systems, a point-of-sale company that operated about 60 percent of the car wash sites in the United States. For a time I sat on DRB's board and knew and respected the people involved. After about six months of golf, I was more than ready to listen.

"Stu, I bought into a three-store car wash chain. A couple young guys built it on a shoestring budget, but now they've borrowed money and maxed out their credit cards. Can you help us?"

"What's the name of the company?" I asked.

"Sgt. Clean."

I flew to Cleveland to visit the business, and I liked what I saw. It was a very small start-up but well run by a couple hardworking guys who immediately became friends. They understood that I'd been an operator for a long time, and they needed my experience. They also needed investment capital. The proposition was straightforward: would I be willing to join them as CEO and make an investment that would help build the company?

"I've learned so much since we started at Texaco. What good is that knowledge if I retire? Wouldn't it be better if I stay active and share what I know with these guys and others?"

"The Stu Crum business bible: inspiration and perspiration."

"I'm motivated by bringing people together."

"It's my mission."

"It's just so exciting to make things grow!"

Once our decision was made, I wrote a check as an investor, which also gave me equity and shares in the business. I say "I" wrote the check, but it was Mia's investment too. Then I took over operation of the business and started commuting again.

I rented an apartment in Cleveland, where I would stay for two weeks at a time, then return to Houston for a week. Three months into that routine, we purchased another car wash—our fourth. Onward!

But lo and behold, early in 2019, my phone rang again. It wasn't a headhunter, the typical means of reaching out and teasing new opportunities. The caller was a managing director at Goldman Sachs.

The gentleman explained that he had received my name as someone who was an experienced corporate leader with operations success in the car wash arena. Then he said, "We've recently purchased a business and removed the CEO. We would like to speak to you about running True Blue Car Wash."

Feast or famine is a cliché, of course. Yet it speaks to cycles. Ups and downs. Victories and defeats. You can experience (and survive) many cycles in just one job or relationship or through a long ascent and steep decline in business, education, science, politics—and love. Let me tell ya.

The Goldman Sachs call was, for me, a blend of two things:

1. *Natural order:* You do good work, and someone eventually notices.
2. *Living your intentions:* You clearly define your plan, keep it in mind, then take action and let the chips fall where they may.

Investment bankers are among the smartest, most academically accomplished people in the world, with advanced degrees from this nation's finest universities. But . . .

. . . What do they know about *operations*?

Let's get serious about your intentions.

Where do you fit in? Do you participate in a business or creative environment where you are king or queen? You may not be top dog, so to speak, and perhaps you'll never be CEO. Yet you excel in your expertise as an auto mechanic, school teacher, carpenter, or stay-at-home mom, and therefore you are *indispensable* even in the company of people with highfalutin academic degrees and other admirable, and maybe even intimidating, accomplishments. Simply stated, your intention is to rise and shine and be recognized and compensated for what you contribute in your home or workplace.

I'm no different. Goldman Sachs did not call me to ask whether I would be interested in becoming the Once and Future King. They needed Stu Crum, who could help them kick a game-winning field goal with proven skills.

When I accepted the True Blue CEO position, I began another listening tour. Through my whole career I have practiced MBWO: "managing by walking around." I drove to each car wash site and visited with all the employees and managers. It was obvious that the company lacked a playbook. There were no processes or systems in place. True Blue would make its new owners much more money once each site functioned efficiently.

Once again, my mandate was change, just as it had been during my Bridgestone tenure. This required me to let go of the chief operating officer, vice president of operations, and head of marketing. For the next two years I took the helm and ran operations until I could find the right people to hire.

But what about Sgt. Clean? Did I cut and run?

Although I left Cleveland, my investment stayed. Two years later, the company was purchased, and I received a payout on my capital.

This is not a boast. It could have gone the other way. The point is my intention was to be involved in private equity ventures, and that required me to grit my teeth and take a risk. Service King had been a disappointment. Sometimes the runner stumbles. Then Sgt. Clean came along and picked me up.

True to My Word

I had done well within established corporations, Texaco, Shell, and Bridgestone. Now I faced a new challenge. Could I join a fledgling operation and help expand it so that ownership could sell the whole bundle at a profit? True Blue was a terrific opportunity to prove myself.

But the new operation was headquartered in Scottsdale, Arizona. I could not ask Mia to move with me to another state so that I could prove I belonged in the private equity arena. Nor did I ever give serious thought about making that request. The decision had been made years before in Miami.

By the time I took the Latin America assignment, my daughter, Katherine, was 13 years old, and our family had relocated eight times. One day she posed a question.

"Daddy, every time we have phone visits with my grandparents, I realize I've never been able to have them close so I can see them a lot. We've always lived so far away."

She reminded me of the distant places we had lived, then she asked a question.

"If I ever get married and have children, will you and Mom live close to me so that my children can have a relationship with their grandparents?"

I was surprised. How many 13-year-old girls think this way? How many already see their future and want to shape it?

I would accept the position with True Blue. But there would be no more relocations. That was the commitment I made to Katherine on that day 20 years before. Houston was our last stop unless my family chose another place.

Katherine is now 33 years old. She's a mother of two and a wife. Clayton is the father of two and a husband. Mia and I spend a lot of time with our grandchildren.

I am now 64 years old and on the move. Every Monday morning I get on an airplane and fly to our new headquarters in Tempe, Arizonia. Every Thursday afternoon I fly back to Houston. It's not heroic, and I don't always love going to the airport. It's a sacrifice. I'd rather hop in my car and drive to the office then be home in time for dinner.

But I made a choice, and I must honor my commitment.

On the other hand, I do enjoy being part of the True Blue team.

When I accepted the job, we had about 150 employees. We now have close to 700. We had 27 locations. We now have 71.

The goal of Goldman Sachs was not merely to grow bigger, nor did the firm intend to wait a decade before making a sale. Private equity ventures are on a short leash. Haste makes waste, but clear intentions allowed us to steadily move forward. True Blue began with $25 million in revenue. A few years later, we sold the enterprise at $100 million in revenue.

Private equity is all about creating value for your shareholders—and for yourself. That equation creates a special incentive in an entrepreneur. Goldman Sachs engineered another successful acquisition, but they also shared their bounty with me.

But by now you know that Mia and I define our wealth as God's money. It is not a game of who wins the most toys. Our earnings would help fund nonprofits and other community ventures. In short, we would be able to better define our ultimate goal:

Legacy.

STU SPEAK

Serving others, or an ideal or a movement or a business deal, is transformational. It raises the spirit like nothing else can, and therefore any personal growth you experience is exponential.

THE INTENTIONAL PLAYBOOK
WHEN THE WRONG GUY GETS IT RIGHT

We laugh about it now, and we're friends. But before I was chosen to lead True Blue, Lynne Berreman was named our chief financial officer by Goldman Sachs. To be blunt, she was quite sure I was the wrong guy for the job.

I could see her point. The Bridgestone division I was formerly running was a $4-billion business unit, and I had a team of 23,000 people helping me make good. In Lynne's opinion, I was living on Easy Street. After our interview, Lynne told her people at Goldman Sachs, "Hey, don't hire this guy. He hasn't worked that hard in the last few years."

When you join a small entrepreneurial company, say goodbye to amenities. You make your own plane reservations. You create your own PowerPoint presentations. You don't have assistants anymore. Not to mention I was 58 years young. Did the kid still have it him?

Intentions. Did I think, "I'll prove her wrong"?

No.

Intentions. I thought, "I will create a plan that includes a listening tour and then trust myself to make bold decisions to help True Blue achieve its goals."

When shaping a plan, I avoid "I want XYZ," because it suggests an emptiness I must fill. When I announce, "I intend to achieve XYZ," I've dropped negative baggage and am free to move forward—immediately.

Despite my age, I was more than willing to do the work: I took on three major positions in the early days just to make sure we got it right.

Did my intention succeed? Well, once I was hired, Lynne shed her doubts and became an indispensable teammate whose skills were essential to our victory. Proving her wrong was not the goal or the outcome. And since there was nothing negative in my approach, we could collaborate. We soon learned that our personalities and skills were complementary. We excelled together.

18

LIFE BEGINS AT 60

When I was 30 years old and Katherine had just been born, Texaco placed me in a variety of positions to test my mettle. I started in a field job running stores, then I went to real estate before being assigned to a human resources position. It was there that I met a project consultant who was 60 years old. I learned a lot from him as we got to know each other, but not what you might expect.

First, this man was a hard worker throughout his life. He scrimped and saved and sacrificed all kinds of pleasures because he had a vision. When he retired—and he was close to that milestone—he planned to build a dream house and live happily ever after in retirement.

He fulfilled his goal. He retired, built the house of his dreams, and then died six months later. He worked his whole life for retirement and never got to enjoy it.

After our time in New Zealand, we returned to the United States, and I was assigned a global marketing role with Texaco. I was pushing 40 when I noticed a gentleman who had a very rigid routine. Every morning he arrived promptly at the office at 6:00, he ate his lunch at noon, and at 3:30 p.m. he left for the day. This was his unwavering routine Monday through Friday. I was perplexed. Didn't he enjoy any aspect of his work? Then it dawned on me: he watched the clock because he was counting the minutes until he could retire.

During my years with Shell, the company promised retirement with full benefits based on an equation: your age plus years of service must equal 80 points. Often I heard some staff members say, "I can't wait until I get my points." Isn't there more to our working years than wishing and hoping for that day when we don't have to work?

I have not lived life to retire. In fact, the one time I did retire—from pro football—it was painful.

Early in our marriage Mia and I decided we would live life as fully as possible and not save every penny for retirement. This didn't mean that we were careless with our income. Retirement would eventually happen, and we knew we had to plan to be financially secure. In the meantime, what about fun, impacting the lives of others, travel, volunteering our time, taking a few risks?

I'm not knocking those who look forward to retirement. It looks different for a lot of different people. I have friends who have gladly left their days of work behind and are pleased with a relaxed, post-career lifestyle.

But when True Blue was sold and I received my share of the equity, I was both elated and introspective. I stayed on as CEO to run the business.

STILL GROWING AFTER ALL THESE YEARS

There were two buyers in the True Blue deal. A small operator in the Northeast, a car dealership, bought six locations. The majority, 65 locations, went to the publicly traded Couche-Tard, a Canadian company headquartered in Montreal that owned Circle K. We now have 66 stores, with a number under construction.

How the deal came about is one clue as to why I'm still in the game.

After four productive years, Goldman Sachs had achieved its goal. New sites had been acquired and built, revenue was expanded, and now it was time to exit the car wash business, which was the intention all along. The sales process was then handed off to the Goldman Sachs investment banking firm that marketed the business.

As the sale process progressed, I received a call from a man who years before had worked for me and now did some contract work for Circle K.

"Hey, Stu, you're in the car wash business, right?"

Affirmative. He continued.

"You know what? Circle K is interested in getting in the car wash business."

"That's really interesting because we happen to be for sale right now," I said.

Coincidence? Fate?

This is what I know: when you stay in the game, good things can happen.

I continued. "Let me speak to Brian."

In 2006 I was head of mergers and acquisitions for Shell Retail in North America. At that time, I became acquainted with Brian Hannasch, a senior vice president in charge of western North America for Circle K. We enjoyed working with one another and negotiated a deal between our respective companies.

And we stayed in touch. That's why 17 years later I knew that Brian was now CEO of Circle K and his firm was one of the largest convenience store companies in the world—and the most valuable.

Brian and I jumped on the phone for an hour and caught up. I learned that his group believed that the car wash arena would be an excellent ancillary profit center to their convenience stores. By the end of the call, he decided to ask his team to appraise the deal. Six months later we signed an agreement.

Relationships matter, and if they are nurtured, there is no way of calculating their true value—and not just in business terms. Business is merely a method for like minds to merge and prosper and blossom on many levels. The opportunities I'm experiencing now could not have happened when I first started with Texaco. And I relish these experiences because they are as sweet as a late-game score at the University of Tulsa.

MENTOR ME

When Goldman Sachs hired me to lead True Blue, they also introduced me to a board member who became a mentor. Me? At my age? Absolutely. At every stage of growth, a mentor can be an exhilarating way to get ahead and succeed at new plateaus.

This relationship is another clue as to why I won't retire—yet.

I knew that my mentor, who is about 10 years older than me, was a formidable man whose résumé was the envy of many businesspeople. But he surprised me with a confession that shed new light on aspirations, retirement rituals, and expanding wealth.

"Stu, listen—I'm just going to share something with you. I've created my own family office, and I built this business after I turned 60. So don't think that life ends at 60; life just begins at 60. And this is when some of your most critical earning years are possible, if you choose that to be."

A family office is a wealth management strategy that is often set up after liquidating a lucrative business or other asset. It helps preserve, expand, and control your assets, rather than hand them off to an investment firm. In short, your wealth is your business.

My mentor's comments were a perfect match for my decision to challenge myself by embracing private equity and other concepts that were new to me. After all, when I was with Texaco, Shell, and Bridgestone, I was acquiring skills. At 60-ish, I took stock of the many formative experiences I had endured and concluded that I had finally acquired, to some degree, that mystical and mythical thing we call wisdom. Why stop now?

But don't get me wrong. Goldman Sachs and then Circle K did not choose me as CEO because I had the financial acumen of Lynne Berreman, for example, whose money IQ was off the charts and essential to the expansion of True Blue. No, each firm understood what Stu Crum brought to the game: leadership.

After 14 years as either CEO or president of a corporation, I have shifted into a new phase. Yes, I still have operational responsibilities, such as profit and loss, at True Blue. But I've put my focus on mentoring and coaching, in particular new CEOs.

How do you learn to be an effective CEO? The men and women I mentor are in their 30s, 40s, and 50s and therefore mature, with plenty of business experience.

Yet giving board presentations on a quarterly basis can be a rough road to hoe if you're not prepared. The meetings can be contentious and tough if the business isn't performing. So I coach the CEOs on how to respond and prepare them for the types of questions they may be asked. They must learn how to maneuver because boards include investors who naturally want to protect their money.

Also, investment bankers are very smart people. At a financial level, they are brighter than bright. At an operational level, it is not their expertise, because they typically do not operate companies on a daily basis.

So the CEO must give them details, clarifications, and a bit of instruction, especially if they are focusing on the wrong indicators and therefore asking questions that are irrelevant. There were times in my career when I had to tell the board where to focus their attention, such as toward the things that truly impact business performance.

Not that members should ignore what seems to be a company downturn or disruption. Economies happen. Recessions happen. Presidential elections happen and wars too. In those events, the CEO must be ready to address those concerns.

Sometimes the CEO must also recognize a blind spot.

In New Zealand 25 years ago, I was head of retail and part of a leadership team that did the strategic planning for our company. At the time there were only four players in our sector—BP, Exxon Mobil, Shell, and us, Caltex—and there was only one oil refinery. Since each company used that refinery exclusively, we determined that there was no opportunity for a new competitor to barge in and take a portion of our market.

Well, guess what? An Australian company announced that they intended to enter our territory by using barges to ship refined products into the country. It was an ingenious idea because it meant that they could bypass our refinery. Suddenly, we had a new competitor that none of us had anticipated.

CEOs can count on one basic truth: *there will always be a disrupter.*

Did Kmart not see Walmart coming?

Was Blockbuster lazy in not analyzing that Netflix was a game changer?

Why did Kodak, a global mainstay, suddenly falter? Apparently, they did not anticipate the iPhone.

Not to mention, did you hail an Uber car today? Or do you prefer the Lyft app?

The CEOs I mentor know that I will tell them that they must have a plan. I bang that drum often. Then I say that they must also be nimble and quick.

As a CEO I weathered many ups and downs. Through the years I've learned that when investors shout "The sky is falling," that probably is not true.

Equally concerning is a sudden rise in value, otherwise known as success. A new CEO might assume that these are the best of times, and it is true: they are electrifying. But don't get too comfortable.

A CEO is always zigging and zagging as best-laid plans are challenged by complications and unexpected global turns of events. The plan keeps you centered, in business and in everyday life. It will likely be revised at some point, but you don't want to be making it up on the spot.

During my first three and a half years with True Blue, I was the smartest guy on the planet. Business was going well, we were booming, and the board loved me. Six months before our exit, the industry sagged, and there was some softness in the car wash arena. I went from being the smartest guy in the galaxy to the dumbest. I could feel the heat, because our investors had real money—*their* money—in the game, and they started second-guessing our plan. Nothing had really changed, though. We found a buyer, and a sale was negotiated.

Facing adversity goes with the territory. That's why a 90-day plan is essential. It answers a critical question: what is the thesis, or long-term ambition of the company? Sometimes a new CEO will be surprised when I look further down the road and ask, "What does an exit, a sale of this business, look like?" I listen to the details, then ask, "How are you going to get there?"

I might ask the same questions of you, the reader. We all aspire. But do you have a plan? If so, have you broken it down into small steps that will help you reach your destination?

Without intentions, we drift, in life and in business. We go to work every day and maybe dream of retirement, but how will that unfold? Without a plan, any road will take you somewhere into the future. But the results may not be fulfilling.

Be transparent.

A new CEO I mentored had a well-thought-out 90-day plan that impressed me. There was only one problem: he didn't share it with anybody. The board was frustrated because they didn't understand why the CEO was steering a certain course. All of this could have been avoided, of course. Don't hunker down alone, trying to perfect an approach that might benefit from some objectivity and other voices.

This may sound simplistic. Believe me: simple works when you are leading a complex corporate entity or designing your own career.

When I was a kid kicking a football through the uprights, I never could have imagined that I'd be leading the charge on such a large scale as an adult. But that kid was resolute. He could take the pressure. In good or bad weather, he knew that his aim was true.

Opening Doors

In 2023 Mia and I mingled with a large group of people on a Friday night in Houston, and yet, for once, the event was not a Texas football game under bright lights. We were at home.

For years our family attended an established church in town, and we remain active there. But once Katherine and Clayton married and began their own families, they joined a new start-up church. We opened our doors for their Christmas celebration, which embraced our true belief that all blessings are to be shared.

It wasn't a difficult decision. Mia and I concluded that if we are the only two people allowed to enjoy our beautiful home, we are wasting God's resources. The house must be part of our ministry. Months later, we hosted a huge fundraiser for a local nonprofit organization.

Private equity is a way of supporting new ventures with the hope that, eventually, everyone involved will make financial and professional gains. By opening our doors, Mia and I are gladly investing in a different way: with our hearts. When all is said and done, when career aspirations and family responsibilities have been fulfilled, Mia and I hope to be remembered simply as generous people.

As I mentor businesspeople, athletes, and people of faith, I am often struck by one universal truth: the uprights are always available to us, in every personal or professional endeavor. And the message they send is clear and eternal.

Aim high.

STU SPEAK

Trust in the Lord with all your heart and lean not unto your own understanding, in all you ways acknowledge him and he will direct your paths.

—Proverbs 3:5–6

THE INTENTIONAL PLAYBOOK
YOUR 90-DAY PLAN

We all want to succeed. Yet vague ambitions, unconscious wishes, and complex game plans can sink the ship. To begin, let's keep it simple by limiting our time frame.

List what you must or would like to accomplish in the next 90 days.

- Include the most mundane and demanding tasks in your professional and personal life.

- After each task, write an intention that begins with, "I intend to . . ." Sometimes the best intentions are merely a shift in attitude, such as completing a task without resenting it.

- Share the intentions that require collaboration. Your spouse, friend, or boss might have useful suggestions.

- Read the intention before you begin, then observe how it makes you feel. Often, when I'm on track and respecting my intention, I'm relaxed or excited about what I'll achieve. Clarity has that power.

- Jot down what you experienced after completing the task. How did it go? Did you stay on track? If not, why? Your feelings are important. Intend to keep track of them.

- Define the uprights that define how to aim your intentions.

The 90-Day Plan includes intentions that will be fulfilled quickly, while others may take weeks or months.

For long-term tasks, create a subset of intentions.

- Start with the central intention.

- In anticipation of challenges and roadblocks, create a specific intention that addresses each issue.

- If the central intention involves discovery—information you are searching for and may surprise you—define how you intend to grapple with the impact.

- Define the uprights.

Your 90-Day Plan list will be in flux. It is a living thing, and life happens. Revising intentions is natural and sometimes critical for fulfilling goals.

Toward the end of your first 90 days, make a list of intentions for the next 90-day period. Define what are "follow-through" intentions and what are newly initiated intentions.

Obviously, when we plan for 90 days, we are merely attempting to focus and simplify a method of moving forward. Life goes on, thankfully; therefore, don't hesitate to harvest any ideas and intentions that pop into your head that you know are part of your grand scheme of fulfillment. They, too, will someday fit nicely into a new 90-Day Plan.

THE REVERSE-INTENTIONS METHOD

You may have business or family intentions that do not have a clear fulfillment date on the calendar, like an anniversary or a college graduation day.

In that case, start with the destination in mind and list steps that must be taken to fulfill your ambition.

There will be unknown factors, but once that list is complete to the best of your ability, break it down into 90-day plans. Find the intersections or segues from one plan to the next.

Your 90-Day Plan is not intended to limit you. Rather, it is a method for developing the habit of defining intentions. Only then can you fully appreciate the wonder and profundity of living an intentional life.

Best wishes.

About the Author

When Stu Crum's college football heroics put him on the national radar as a model student-athlete, the expectations for a bright future could not have predicted his soaring ascent in business. Tagged as a winner with a natural gift for leadership, Crum made his name internationally in key positions with Texaco, Shell Oil, Jiffy Lube, and Bridgestone, wrangling deals with the likes of activist investor Carl Icahn and other heavy hitters.

Yet beneath the surface lay a deeper man. While still at University of Tulsa, Crum devoted his life to his faith and embraced servant leadership as his game plan for ultimate success in business, family, faith, and fun. Despite personal setbacks and injury-laden stints with the NFL and USFL, Crum blossomed at every turn by developing a simple, dynamic playbook that put his every aspiration within reach. He calls it intentional living.